TABLE OF CONTENTS

PREFACE i

I. KEY FINDINGS 1

II. INTRODUCTION 5
   Two Roads to the Social Scientific Study of Women in Muslim Cultures 5
   Monolithic Stereotype Succumbs to Multi-Faceted Empirical Studies on Muslim Women.... 9

III. THE SCHOLARSHIP ON WOMEN IN ISLAMIC SOCIETIES 13
   General Features of the Scholarly Literature 13
      Two Interpretive Poles in the Literature 13
      Uneven Representation of Different Regions, Nations, and Classes 15
   Assessing Women's Status: Categories of Data, Categories of Scholarly Work 18
      The Production of Data and Research Tools 18
      Specialized and Microstudies 24
      Consolidation of Knowledge about Women in Islamic Societies 26

IV. DIMENSIONS OF WOMEN'S STATUS AND BODIES OF RESEARCH 27
   Sex-Role Ideologies and Feminist Discourses: Examining Sacred Texts and Contexts 27
   Legal Contexts: Women's Legal Position and Rights 32
      Dual Legal Systems and Family Law Reform: Challenging the Substance of Laws 33
      Muslim Family Law in Contemporary and Historical Practice 41
   Demographics, Health, and Education: Ongoing "Sociological Modernization" 46
      The Demographic Picture 47
      Beyond Demography's Limits 55
   Marriage, Family, Household, and Everyday Life 56
      The Neopatriarchal Family and the Role of the State 58
      Attitudes and Actualities: The Neopatriarchal Family 60
      The New Work on Taboo Subjects: Violence and Female Circumcision 64
   Women and the Productive Economy: Necessity or Empowerment? 71
      When Women Go to Market: Women in Paid Labor in Muslim Societies 73
      Structural Features That Explain the Labor Force Experience of Muslim Women 77
      Studies on Women's Participation in the Informal Economy 80
      Microlevel Empirical Field Studies 83
   Women in Muslim States and Politics 87
      Formal Politics: Office-Holding and Electoral Politics 87
      Women's Activism for Building the Nation, Development, and Human/Women's
         Rights 91

V. CONCLUSION 93

SELECTED BIBLIOGRAPHY 95

I. KEY FINDINGS

General Observations

- More than half a billion of the women in the world are Muslim. They are concentrated in approximately 45 Muslim-majority countries in a broad belt from Senegal to the Philippines, with the largest number on the South Asian subcontinent. The most populous single Muslim-majority nation is Indonesia.

- Monolithic stereotypes of Muslim women have long prevailed in the West, distorting the enormous interregional, intraregional, and class variations in their circumstances and status.

- Serious social scientific scholarship on women worldwide was scarce until the 1970s. Since then the study of women, including Muslim women, has exploded. The social science literature on Muslim women is now voluminous and growing.

- The Western understanding of Muslim women remains unduly influenced by evidence from a single region. The social science scholarship most familiar to the West about Muslim women focuses disproportionately on the Middle East and North Africa region (MENA). Often seen as the land of Muslims par excellence, MENA is home to fewer than 20 percent of the world's Muslims.

- Women in Muslim societies and communities face gender-based inequalities associated with the so-called "patriarchal gender system." Aspects of this originally pre-capitalist system persist in rural areas across a wide swath of lands, both Muslim and non-Muslim, from East Asia to North Africa. The system, regardless of religion, features kin-based extended families, male domination, early marriage (and consequent high fertility), restrictive codes of female behavior, the linkage of family honor with female virtue, and occasionally, polygamous family structure. In Muslim areas, veiling and sex-segregation form part of the gender system.

- Most current scholarship rejects the idea that the Islamic religion is the primary determinant of the status and conditions of Muslim women. Because of the wide variation in Muslim women's status and conditions, researchers typically attribute more causal salience to determining factors that themselves vary across nations and regions. To account for the variable situations of Muslim women, scholars cite as causal factors, for example, variations in the economic structures and strategies of nations, or variations in the preexisting cultural value patterns of a given locale.

- The sacred writings of Islam, like those of the other Abrahamic faiths—Christianity and Judaism—have been interpreted in ways that support patriarchal social relations. Until the last two decades, Western observers of the plight of Muslim women have portrayed Islam as uniquely patriarchal and incompatible with women's equality. Most scholars now see Islam as no more inherently misogynist than the other major monotheistic traditions.

PREFACE

Half a billion Muslim women inhabit some 45 Muslim-majority countries, and another 30 or more countries have significant Muslim minorities, including, increasingly, countries in the developed West. This study provides a literature review of recent empirical social science scholarship that addresses the actualities of women's lives in Muslim societies across multiple geographic regions. The study seeks simultaneously to orient the reader in the available social scientific literature on the major dimensions of women's lives and to present analyses of empirical findings that emerge from these bodies of literature. Because the scholarly literature on Muslim women has grown voluminous in the past two decades, this study is necessarily selective in its coverage. It highlights major works and representative studies in each of several subject areas and alerts the reader to additional significant research in lengthy footnotes.

In order to handle a literature that has grown voluminous in the past two decades, the study includes an "Introduction" and a section on "The Scholarship on Women in Islamic Societies" that offer general observations—bird's eye views—of the literature as a whole. The Introduction describes the two main sources of the social scientific studies on women in Muslim communities, namely, 1) academic programs on women worldwide that emerged under the impetus of post-1970s women's movements and 2) international and national economic development agencies that came to see women's disadvantaged status as a hindrance to development. It also describes the broad thrust of the social scientific literature on various spheres or dimensions of Muslim women's lives: ideology, law, family, economy, and politics.

"The Scholarship on Women in Islamic Societies" section describes features that pervade the entire literature. One feature is that the studies tend to align themselves on a spectrum between two interpretive poles, one relatively negative, the other positive, about the situation of women in Islamic societies. The second feature is that the literature is highly uneven in its coverage, with a disproportionate representation, in particular, of the Middle East and North Africa region. It also discusses the sources of the primary data upon which researchers draw in studies across a variety of fields and describes two types of work that make up the literature on women in Muslim societies, specialized microstudies and projects of consolidation.

The final section "Dimensions of Women's Status and Bodies of Research" characterizes the bodies of literature that have developed to illuminate particular dimensions of women's lives. This portion covers, in separate sections, the substantial bodies of social scientific work that have developed on each of the following major dimensions of women's experience and condition: religious ideology, law, demography, family, economics, and politics.

- Many cultural practices associated with Islam and criticized as oppressive to women are misidentified as "Islamic." Controversial or egregious practices such as female circumcision, polygamy, early marriage, and honor killings are not limited to Muslim populations, and among Muslims such practices are geographically specific or otherwise far from universal.

The Legal Context: Women's Legal Position and Rights

- The legal systems under which women live in Muslim countries are mostly dual systems. They consist, on the one hand, of civil law, which is indebted to Western legal systems, and on the other hand, of family or personal status law, which is mainly built upon Sharia, Islamic religious-based law. The civil law as well as the constitutions of many Muslim states provide for equal rights between women and men. However, Islamic family law as variously manifested in Muslim nations poses obstacles to women's equality.

- Islamic family law, which addresses marriage, divorce, child custody, and inheritance, has long been a target for reform. Many state elites have pressed for family law reform to further state interests by removing hindrances to women's full participation in the labor force and politics.

- Reforms of family law often have been limited by the state's perceived need to appease conservative social elements and, since the 1970s, growing Islamist movements. Islamist movements, sometimes through outright state takeover, as in Iran, occasionally have succeeded in rolling back "women-friendly" reforms previously achieved.

- Family law reforms continue, often thanks to the pressure of proliferating groups of Muslim activists for women rights. In 2004, a major success was the overhaul of conservative family law in Morocco, which now boasts a relatively progressive system.

- In many Muslim states, the substance of family law and its actual implementation differ in ways that somewhat mitigate the gender imbalance of the laws on the books. Women are able and sometimes officially encouraged to exploit rules and loopholes to circumvent discriminatory provisions in the law. Women can, for example, write clauses into marriage contracts that make taking another wife grounds for divorce and for post-divorce division of marital assets. A growing form of feminist activism at present aims to educate women about such strategies and available loopholes.

Demographics, Health, and Education: Ongoing "Sociological Modernization"

- Whatever hindrances to equality Muslim legal systems pose for women, Muslim women across all regions have made rapid progress in recent decades in a number of statistically measurable aspects of life, notably education and health. In these areas, Muslim nations have significantly reduced both gender gaps and the formerly wide differences in average attainment between Muslim and non-Muslim societies. In education, for example, a generation ago women in MENA had among the lowest levels of education in the world. MENA females now have achieved parity with males at some levels of schooling.

- Macro-level statistics also show a rapid reduction in Muslim and non-Muslim differences in reproduction-related behaviors. In the recent past, Muslim women exhibited comparatively high rates of fertility and low rates of contraception use. They now are participating in the worldwide trend of declining fertility. In some cases, such as in Iran, they have attained below-replacement fertility. Iran, in fact, effected the most rapid demographic transition ever seen.

- Viewed in terms of large-scale statistical indicators, Muslim women are becoming ever more like other women. This fact undercuts the assumption that "Islam" would inhibit Muslim women's participation in such worldwide trends as declining childbearing. On average, broad social and economic forces for change override whatever special influence Islam might have.

Marriage, Family, Household, and Everyday Life

- In the sphere of the family, macro-level statistics indicate a shift to a nuclear family from a pattern of extended family and multi-generational households. Statistics also indicate that Muslims are delaying marriage and increasing their rate of non-marriage. Such shifts spell erosion of the traditional kinship-based patriarchal family, which persists as an ideal among conservatives.

- Caught between the traditional patriarchal family model and an egalitarian nuclear model, today's Muslim families have been called "neopatriarchal." They continue to feature intra-familial gender-based inequality.

- Scholarship within the last decade has begun to address the darkest aspects of such familial gender-based inequality, including the hitherto taboo topics of domestic violence, honor killings, and female circumcision. Such charged issues have figured prominently on the agendas of women's rights advocates in Muslim communities since the Fourth World Conference on Women in Beijing in 1995.

Women and the Productive Economy: Necessity or Empowerment?

- Establishing the levels of the labor force participation of Muslim women is a challenge to researchers because a high proportion of women's paid work, as in all developing economies, occurs in the informal economy.

- In at least one heavily Muslim region, namely, MENA, female labor force participation appears to be exceptionally low, although growing. In other Muslim-majority lands, for example, Southeast Asia, it is high.

- The levels of Muslim women's participation in the paid labor force are best explained by a particular economy's development strategy and consequent need for female labor, rather than by, for example, religious ideology or cultural beliefs in male breadwinner/female-homemaker roles. In the oil-boom years prior to the mid-1980s, the oil-centered economies of MENA did not require female labor in order to grow. Thus, oil-rich nations such as Saudi Arabia had few women in the labor force. By contrast,

Muslim counties that sought to develop through labor-intensive industrial production, such as Tunisia, Malaysia, or Indonesia, feature high female labor force participation.

- The globalization of the past quarter century—i.e., the increasing international integration of markets in the global capitalist economy—is a fundamental factor in the evolving role of women in Muslim societies, as in others.

- Globalization increased economic and job insecurity and thus the need for more than one breadwinner in a family. At the same time, in many national economies, globalization has reduced the proportion of formal sector employment, which was in any case out of reach for many Muslim women. Globalization also has prompted the withdrawal of the state from service provision, thereby increasing women's family burdens. The effect of globalization on Muslim women thus often has been increased hardship. At the same time, many women have reported an enhanced sense of empowerment as a result of their enlarged public role and earnings.

Women in Muslim States and Politics

- Women have gained basic political rights—the right to vote and to stand for office—in almost all Muslim-majority states, with the last major holdouts, Kuwait and Saudi Arabia, on the verge of joining the others. Despite having such rights, Muslim women, like women worldwide, are underrepresented in high office and legislatures. However, a number of Muslim countries outside of MENA have seen women in high office in numbers that exceed world averages. Such cases of above-average office-holding generally reflect quota systems and/or the power of family ties in politics.

- Although Muslim women are underrepresented in formal politics, their activism within Muslim states for the advancement of women's rights and interests is widespread and growing. Advocacy and activist groups have proliferated, exhibiting great variety in their political complexion, in their avowal of religious commitment, and in the radicalism of their demands for change.

- In the 1990s, secular feminists and so-called Islamic feminists, formerly at odds, achieved some rapprochement. Secular feminists now recognize value in the other camp's preoccupation with providing woman-friendly "rereadings" of Islam's sacred texts. Justifying feminist activism in Islamic terms shields feminist demands from the charge that they are alien Western impositions. Islamic feminists increasingly see Islamic precepts and universal (e.g., United Nations) articulations of human/women's rights as compatible.

- A significant development for Muslim women's rights activists in the past decade has been the growth of transnational networks, such as Women Living Under Muslim Laws and Sisters in Islam. Exploiting the revolution in communications, these networks advocate legal reform and organize resistance to Islamist threats to women's progress.

II. INTRODUCTION

Two Roads to the Social Scientific Study of Women in Muslim Cultures

Until the latter decades of the twentieth century, the question of women's status and roles in Muslim cultures and societies was profoundly neglected. Western-inspired studies of the Muslim world mentioned women in passing, but in stereotyped and sensationalistic ways, while the bulk of locally produced literature on women in Islam consisted of discussions of the "right" place of women in society, including, at best, didactic manuals on how to live a pious but modern life. Serious empirically based social science research on women and sex-disaggregated data were in short supply. This paucity of rigorous social research began to be remedied in the late 1970s, and by the late 1980s scholarship about women in Muslim societies had truly taken off. The 1990s saw an explosion of writing about women, which is ongoing, as is the growth in the number of interested scholars who address issues of gender and Islam.[1]

The impetus for this burgeoning research and serious coverage of women in Muslim societies came from two quite separate directions. One impetus was the emergence of women's movements worldwide beginning in the 1970s, movements of activists who pushed for women's rights and gender equity. Another impetus came from the economic development interests of national governments and international organizations. Such institutions began to focus on a range of women's issues—initially a narrow range, e.g., fertility limitation and maternal health—as women came to be seen as an element in development.

Women's movements, or activism outside academe, fueled studies within academic settings across an array of academic disciplines, including the social sciences. Social scientists within the various disciplines each adopted the multiple goals of remedying women's "invisibility" within the discipline's focus area and of exposing women's unequal status and access to societal goods. Simultaneously, social scientists, in using gender as a major category of analysis, sought to transform and improve their disciplines. As of the 1970s, the discipline of history, for instance, challenged the marginalization of women in the historical record, initially

---

[1] One gauge of the exponential growth in scholarly attention to women in Islamic societies is a two-volume bibliography compiled by Yvonne Haddad and others. The first volume, *The Contemporary Islamic Revival*, which covers works published between 1970 and 1988, needed only eight of its 230 pages to list writing dealing with "Women." In the second volume, *The Islamic Revival Since 1988*, whose 298 pages cover works published between 1988 and 1997, the same category had swelled to 40 pages. Full citations of the volumes are: Yvonne Yazbeck Haddad, John Obert Voll, and John L. Esposito, *The Contemporary Revival: A Critical Survey and Bibliography* (New York: Greenwood Press, 1991); and Yvonne Yazbeck Haddad and John L. Esposito, *The Islamic Revival Since 1988: A Critical Survey and Bibliography* (Westport, CN: Greenwood Publishing, 1997).

recovering elite women—"women worthies"—as part of traditional political history, and later producing innovative anthropologically influenced social history about ordinary women and various aspects of their lives and historical contributions. Sociology built up a substantial body of work about women's roles and status in the family, in education, in the workplace, and in social formations and movements, and examined how gender inequalities are constructed and maintained in the various arenas of life.[2] Even economics, the most resistant of the social science disciplines to addressing the gendered nature of its study area—economic processes—developed, by late 1980s, a sub-field of feminist economics. This sub-field took mainstream economics to task, for example, for studying workers as a generic, sex-undifferentiated category, and for failing to count the value of the world's unpaid or non-marketed production, most of it contributed by women.[3] Feminist economics also questioned standard measures of economic well-being, such as GDP per capita, and proposed alternatives more capable of capturing non-market gains and losses that disproportionately affect women and other marginalized groups.[4]

Such women-focused work in the various social science disciplines initially emerged in the United States and Europe but spread within a decade to venues outside the West, including venues in parts of the Muslim world where women's reform organizations and feminist networks became active.[5] In the wake of this spread of a research interest in women, university programs in women's studies and academic research centers were established in the Muslim world. Leading research centers in the Arab world were formed in Cairo, Egypt, and Beirut, Lebanon.[6]

---

[2] For a discussion of the development of a feminist strand within sociology, see Myra Marx Ferree, Shamus Khan, and Shauna A. Morimoto, "Assessing the Feminist Revolution: The Presence and Absence of Gender in Theory and Practice," June 25, 2005. < http://www.ssc.wisc.edu/~mferree/ferree%20khan%20morimoto%20-%20final.doc>

[3] Representative studies in this sub-field of economics appear in *Feminist Economics*, the journal of the International Association for Feminist Economics (IAFFE), an organization that seeks to advance feminist inquiry of economic issues and to educate economists and others on feminist points of view on such issues. Incorporated in 1992, IAFFE was accorded NGO in special consultative status with the Economic and Social Council of the United Nations in 1997. IAFFE has 600 members, the majority economists, in 43 countries.

[4] For an early discussion of the need for such alternative, gender-sensitve measures of economic well-being, see Marilyn Waring, *Counting for Nothing: What Men Value and What Women are Worth*, 2nd ed. (Toronto: University of Toronto Press. 1999; orig. 1987). Offering a feminist analysis of modern economics, Waring empasizes how woman's housework and care for others is automatically excluded from value in economic theory. See also Marianne A. Ferber and Julie A. Nelson, *Beyond Economic Man: Feminist Theory and Economics* (Chicago: The University of Chicago Press, 1993); Julie Nelson, *Feminism, Objectivity and Economics* (London: Routledge, 1996); and Marianne A. Ferber and Julie A. Nelson, *Feminist Economics Today: Beyond Economic Man* (Chicago: University of Chicago Press, 2003).

[5] For a discussion of the activities of women's movements and feminist networks in the Muslim world, see the section "Women in Muslim States and Politics."

[6] A notable center in Lebanon is the Institute for Women's Studies in the Arab World, Lebanese American University, Beirut. Egypt has numerous research venues on women. On these and other centers, see Saad Eddin

In Jordan, in 2000, a women's studies program was initiated at the faculty of graduate studies of the University of Jordan. In 1995, Palestine established the Institute of Women's Studies at Bir Zeit University. Academic venues in the non-Arab Muslim world also became host to women's studies and research centers.

At the same time that studies began to proliferate and programs to form in academic settings, governments and organizations with an interest in economic development themselves undertook more serious study of women. At first—into the 1970s—such study had limited aims, addressing the "population explosion" and high fertility rates as impediments to modernization and capitalist development. Interested in preventing population growth from offsetting the gains of economic development, governments sponsored national family planning and maternal/child health programs and sought knowledge relevant to women defined primarily as mothers. Gradually the aims of government policy makers broadened as they came to see women as an underutilized resource and, in some regions, particularly Southeast Asia, as a potential source of cheap labor for state-led industrialization and modernization projects. As evidence accumulated that the subordinate status of females impedes development both by hindering population limitation and by reducing women's productive contributions, development organizations began targeting women as beneficiaries of programs; the organizations sought to facilitate women's access to resources and participation in the labor force. Targeting women primarily in the name of efficiency and for the sake of development, governments and state-sponsored development programs eventually also responded to pressures emanating from women's movements to widen further the goals vis-à-vis women, and to make women's rights and empowerment a higher priority.

The same combination of motivation and pressures that affected national governments—development imperatives and women's organized equity demands—led also to greater action and research on women on the international level, in international organizations involved in development assistance, such as the United Nations Development Programme (UNDP) and the United Nations Population Fund (UNFPA), and among donor institutions such as the World Bank and various foundations. Among the results of the greater international interest in women were the first and second United Nations Decades for Women (1976–1995), which encouraged, beginning with the 1975 World Conference on Women (WCW), significant

Ibrahim, "Arab Social-Science Research in the 1990s and Beyond: Issues, Trends, and Priorities" (Canada: International Development Research Centre). <http://www.idrc.ca/en/ev-41625-201-1-DO_TOPIC.html>

global networking on gender issues and fueled demands to incorporate gender awareness into development planning. In the context of the Arab and Muslim world, as elsewhere, the United Nations provided needed support for existing women-based and human rights networks, as well as the impetus for social science research. A series of international conferences, including the 1994 International Conference on Population and Development (ICPD) in Cairo, the 1995 World Summit on Social Development (WSSD) in Copenhagen, and the 1995 Fourth World Conference on Women in Beijing all required participating delegations to provide country and regional studies and energized Arab and non-Arab Muslim social scientists to focus on hitherto neglected topics concerning women. In addition, international legislation such as the Convention for the Elimination of all Forms of Discrimination Against Women (CEDAW) and the Beijing Platform for Action (BPFA), among others, galvanized action and research.[7] Sixteen out of the twenty-two Arab countries signed (CEDAW), as did most other Muslim-majority nations.[8]

The Beijing Platform called for women-centered programs and for "mainstreaming" women in all existing and future development projects. The aspiration to "mainstream" women obliged member and aid recipient governments to keep track of the status and progress of women. Within multilateral and bilateral aid agencies, as of the mid-1970s women-in-development (WID) research and action emerged to address how to increase women's access to development programs and projects and to assess the results.[9] This WID interest and scholarship—later renamed "Gender and Development" (GAD) to suggest a broader agenda—was also pursued by non-governmental organizations (NGO). Often responsible for implementing programs, women-centered NGOs developed research arms. Policy researchers in the WID/GAD framework developed a body of work, including much work in the non-Arab Muslim world, whose emphasis differed from that of academic researchers. Often more

---

[7] For a special issue on CEDAW and Arab countries, see the quarterly journal of the Institute for Women's Studies in the Arab World, Lebanese American University, Beirut, *Al-Raida* 15, nos. 80-81 (Winter/Spring 1998).

[8] United Nations, U.N. Development Fund for Women (UNIFEM), *Progress of Arab Women: One Paradigm, Four Arenas, and More than 140 Million Women*, 2004, 15. <http://www.arabwomenconnect.org/docs/PAW2004-ch1.pdf> Signatories now include 180 nations, some of which signed "with reservations." The Arab signatory countries are Algeria, Comoros Islands, Egypt, Iraq, Jordan, Kuwait, Lebanon, Libya, Morocco, Tunisia, Yemen, and Saudi Arabia, Syria, Bahrain, Djibouti, and Mauritania.

[9] The first WID offices—all sparsely funded—were established within the aid agencies of Sweden (SIDA), 1968, the United States (USAID), 1973, and Norway (NORAD), 1975. The World Bank also had a WID adviser in the mid-1970s. Canada (CIDA) and the Netherlands (DGIS) added WID offices soon after the pioneers.

economic in focus and "applied," this work focuses on the obstacles to, and the practicalities of, increasing women's well-being.[10]

Monolithic Stereotype Succumbs to Multi-Faceted Empirical Studies on Muslim Women

The expansion of scholarship on and by women in Islamic cultures, whether produced in development policy or academic quarters, allows for an ever more subtle appreciation of situations and lived realities of women in many dimensions of their experience and in a variety of geographic and social settings. Recent scholarly production involves unprecedented and wide-ranging engagement with the empirical realities of Muslim societies. A growing body of empirical studies aims to unpack the simplistic, stereotypical assumptions about the conditions for women in the Muslim world and to question the validity of any straightforward causal link between Islam and such conditions. Some researchers, indeed, challenge the value of thinking in terms of Muslim women and use instead regional, national, or ethnic categorizations such as Middle Eastern, Indonesian, or Arab.

Empirical studies are not the only type of scholarly efforts currently appearing on women and Islam. The empirical work has developed alongside another large category of work about and by women, discussion that focuses on Islam as a religion and thought system. Scholarship by women on religious doctrine—the exegesis of theological texts and analysis of religious traditions—now looms large in the expanding body of work on women, because part of understanding and changing the status of women is comprehending and addressing the ideological underpinnings, including religious rationales, that support women's subordination and gender-based inequalities. Religious discussion continues also because of the retention of some religious-based laws in most Muslim-majority societies. The Islamic religion appears to have a particularly direct linkage with legal questions that have been at the forefront of public debates on the status of women.

However, although religious discourse remains a major preoccupation in the new scholarly literature on Muslim women, the empirical work breaks especially fresh ground, examining how women fare in the various concrete spheres or dimensions of their lives.

---

[10] For a 72-page bibliography that covers much of the work about Muslim women produced in development policy contexts, see Joan Nordquist, ed., *Third World Women and Development: A Bibliography* (Santa Cruz, CA: Reference and Research Services, 2001). It is worth noting that this bibliography categorizes women by nations and regions. Like most work of development specialists, it does not deploy the category Muslim women, but speaks of women as, for example, Middle Eastern, Arab, Egyptian, or Indonesian.

Researchers from each of the major social science disciplines and several interdisciplinary areas, such as Middle Eastern and women's studies, have played their part in filling out a more complete picture of women in Islamic societies. The broad areas of investigation, seen through the lenses of various disciplinary paradigms and methods, include law, demography and public health, marriage and family, economic life, and politics. Prominent themes are women's disadvantage under Islamic law and how this plays out in practice; rapid demographic change, including declining fertility and increasing marriage age; decreasing gender disparities in education; the prevalence of gender-based violence; Islamic dress and veiling (*hijab*); below average but growing female labor-force participation; under-representation in political decision-making; and the impact of "fundamentalism" and feminism on the status and well-being of women.

Considered together, the empirical studies document the persistence in Muslim societies of features of what many social scientists call the patriarchal gender system. At the same time, the studies document marked and often rapid change in women's roles, status, and well-being, as well as enormous cross-national, cross-regional and sub-national diversity. Along with documenting trends, the research community, in an on-going explanatory enterprise, devotes itself to identifying and weighing the determinants of the trends described.

In describing the persistence of features associated with patriarchal gender systems, researchers of Muslim societies often point out that the features in question are prominent across the entire so-called "belt of classic patriarchy."[11] The patriarchal gender system was originally associated with precapitalist forms of social organization and remains in evidence in rural areas across a wide swath of Asia and North Africa. The patriarchal belt stretches from North Africa across the Muslim Middle East (including non-Arab Turkey and Iran) to South and East Asia (Pakistan, Afghanistan, northern India, and rural China). The belt, regardless of religion, is characterized by kin-based patrilineal extended families, male domination, early marriage (and consequent high fertility), son preference, restrictive codes of behavior for women, and the association of family honor with female virtue. Occasionally, the family structure is polygamous. In the Muslim areas of the patriarchal belt, veiling and sex-segregation, legitimated by appeal to the Qur'an and other sacred writings, form part of the gender system. In some

---

[11] See John C. Caldwell, *Theory of Fertility Decline* (London: Academic Press, 1982); and Deniz Kandiyoti, "Bargaining with Patriarchy," *Gender and Society*, 2, no. 3 (September 1988): 274–90.

Muslim areas, too, the preoccupation with female virginity leads to severe sanctions, including even honor killings, for perceived sexual misconduct by women.[12]

In describing such persistent features of patriarchy, particularly the lack of full equality within families and marriage, researchers underscore the features of life that make certain Muslim societies and social segments most distinctive when compared with urbanized capitalist communities, Muslim and otherwise. Researchers, who are often scholar-activists, typically highlight such features with the aim of exposing realities that place a drag on development and/or compromise the well-being of women. At the same time, serious researchers all recognize that the persistence of such features is a matter of degree. Everywhere they see evidence of movement away from them, albeit at various rates. Social scientists who focus on the Muslim world are unanimous in emphasizing the non-uniformity, at present and historically, of the features of "classic patriarchy" across regions, nations, and sub-national segments of society. Women in Muslim societies, in key dimensions of their lives, currently partake of the same broad trends as women in non-Muslim nations, the trends that accompany the movement from so-called "traditional" roles and societies to more "modern" roles and societies. Among these trends are demographic changes, such as the decline in childbearing (and acceptance of modern contraception) and delays in marriage. Muslim women of whatever region—e.g., the Middle East and North Africa (MENA), South Asia, and Southeast Asia—are more likely than in previous generations to plan and limit their families and to postpone marriage. Certain nations, including the conservative Islamic Republic of Iran, have seen not only the "demographic transition" from high to low fertility, but, with startling rapidity, have also recently achieved below-replacement birth rates. Another general trend is change in family structure and increased likelihood of living in a nuclear, as opposed to a multi-generational household. Gender gaps in education are decreasing. In Arab countries, substantial investments in education aimed at improving women's productive potential have eliminated the gap at some levels, and in Southeast Asia, women's secondary school enrollment has increased dramatically since 1960. In the latter region, more markedly than in Arab lands, women have also participated in another worldwide trend: they account for steadily increasing proportions of total labor force growth, with fewer in agriculture and more in clerical positions.

---

[12] Valentine M. Moghadam, "Patriarchy in Transition: Women and the Changing Family in the Middle East," *Journal of Comparative Family Studies*, 35 no. 2 (2004): 137–63.

The documentation of such large-scale trends as they affect Muslim women serves as a starting point in the expanding body of social scientific work on women in Islamic societies. Most researchers seek to go beyond the identification of general trends. They seek as well to advance understanding of the dynamics at work to produce the change and variability in women's positions and to contribute to the in-depth comprehension of women's lives in all their variety. As in social science work generally, the work on women in Islamic societies moves beyond the mere description of women's positions and situations via two research approaches: qualitative and quantitative research investigations.

Qualitative research studies, conducted by anthropologists, make up the bulk of empirical work on Muslim women. They involve fieldwork and other data-collection techniques such as participant observation, oral histories, and interviews. These ethnographies illuminate the actual aspirations and self-understandings of women, as well as the strategies they devise to counter and/or cope with their often-limiting circumstances.

By contrast, quantitative research studies go beyond mere description of social phenomena by seeking to sort out causal and/or correlational patterns among various factors, for example, economics, religious affiliation, and cultural values. Typical research topics about Muslim women include whether religious beliefs have a significant impact on, for example, fertility behavior or on economic decisions such as entry into the formal labor market. In taking up such questions, researchers face the central challenges of "explanation" in the social sciences, determining what influences what and to what degree. With respect to seeing religion as a primary determinant either of particular behaviors or of women's status broadly, many researchers find it equally plausible that causality runs in the other direction, with, for example, economic outcomes or fertility decisions spurring religious adaptation. Many underscore the salience of structural determinants other than religion. In the research on Muslim women as elsewhere, when researchers assert the primacy of one factor over another, they often find themselves elevating their own scholastic specialty as a primary factor, as when economists assert the primacy of economic development or the world system over religion, or sociologists find that preexisting cultural value patterns of a given locale or sub-group trump religious affiliation, so that religion is the result of such patterns as much as their cause. Social scientists also seek to cope with the complexity of explaining behavior by utilizing various quantitative tools and statistical methods that can cope with systematic analyses involving multiple variables. Most highly developed in conventional economics, one of these methods includes finding the correlation coefficients between several outcomes such as literacy and fertility rates and performing regression analyses to assign different weights to a variety of causes.[13]

Both approaches—qualitative and quantitative research studies—that explore microlevel and macrolevel trends are well represented in the literature concerning women in Islamic societies.

III. THE SCHOLARSHIP ON WOMEN IN ISLAMIC SOCIETIES

Whatever the approach and whatever the area of investigation, there are a number of general points to bear in mind concerning the large body of social science literature about women in Islamic societies. Pertinent to the entire literature, these points are in a broad sense political. The first noteworthy point is that the literature manifests an interpretive division or tug-of-war between two camps, one camp that wishes to absolve Islam as such from blame for women's low status and another camp that finds defensiveness about Islam to be a trap, luring scholars into undue "buy-in" to conservative rationales for gender inequity and away from recognizing a secular stance as the only basis for positive change. The second point that needs to be borne in mind is the unevenness of the coverage of the literature, whereby, for loosely "political' reasons, some regions, nations, and sub-national groups draw much more attention from scholars than others.

General Features of the Scholarly Literature

Two Interpretive Poles in the Literature

Taking the first point, writings on the topic of women and Muslim societies tend to arrange themselves on a spectrum between two interpretive poles. Non-scholarly expressions of the two poles would be, on the one hand, apologetics about women's lives that come from within conservative/fundamentalist Muslim camps, and on the other hand, "Orientalist" sensationalism about how completely oppressive Islam is to women.[14] Scholarly and social scientific work on aspects of women's status avoids the blatancy of either pole, but is similarly fissured along lines

---

[13] For an example of such methods applied to questions about Muslim women, see Jennifer Olmsted, "Reexamining the Fertility Puzzle in the Middle East and North Africa," 73–92, in Eleanor Doumato and Marsha Pripstein-Posusney, eds., *Women and Globalization in the Arab Middle East: Gender, Economy and Society* (Boulder: Lynne Rienner, 2003).

of relatively positive and relatively negative "takes" on what is happening to women in Muslim societies and whether Islam bears responsibility.

The more positive accounts about women, often by feminist Muslim scholars, manifest the impulse to counter ethnocentrism and the perceived Western bias of blanket, negative portrayal of women's status, as well as the tendency to blame unequal status and curtailed rights on Islam. Scholars in this sympathetic camp tend to argue that Islam is not inherently oppressive to women and to counter Islam-bashing by emphasizing that factors other than Islam play a large role in the realities of women's lives.[15] To the extent that women are disadvantaged relative to men, the source of women's subjugation is variously identified as, for example, patriarchal social relations that pre-existed Islam and shaped its development and legal spin-offs, or structural factors and general trends in the world's political economy. For example, Valentine Moghadam, a political economist of Iranian background, argues that women's low labor force participation in the Middle East and North Africa reflects the functioning of oil economies, more than of Islam.[16] Anthropologist Mounira Charrad compares the status of women in three North African countries, Morocco, Algeria, and Tunisia, and attributes the differing patterns of women's sociopolitical participation and access to legal rights not so much to Islam as to the ways in which kinship systems in the societies affected—differentially—the process of state building.[17] Other scholars, especially anthropologists, who predominate among scholars working on women and Islam, counter blanket negativism about women's experience by emphasizing the ways in which women manage, despite restrictions, to maneuver in society to subvert oppressive practices and

---

[14] On "Orientalism, see Chandra Talpate Mohanty, "Under Western Eyes: Feminist Scholarship and Colonial Discourses," 51–80, in Chandra Talpate Mohanty, et al., eds., *Third World Women and the Politics of Memory* (Bloomington : Indiana University Press, 1991).

[15] Scholars in this sympathetic camp include academic supporters of what some have called Islamic feminism, a term from which many feminists so named shy away. According to Margot Badran's usage of the term, Islamic feminism is an indigenous development in Muslim lands in the late twentieth century. As she uses the term, Islamic feminism was born in Egypt and Iran within the last two decades and developed elsewhere as well, for example, in Malaysia. Others use the terms more restrictively, referring to developments among Iranian advocates of women's rights in the 1990's. In any case, Islamic feminism is a reaction against Islamism, or political Islam. Islamic feminism deploys religiously grounded discourse in struggling to improve women's rights. See Margot Badran, "Toward Islamic Feminisms: A Look at the Middle East," in Asma Afsaruddin, ed., *Hermeneutics and Honor: Negotiating Female "Public" Space in Islamic/ate Societies.* Cambridge, MA: Center for Middle Eastern Studies, Harvard University Press, 1999. For further discussion, see also sections below, "Sex-Role Ideologies and Feminist Discourses" and Women in Muslim States and Politics."

[16] See Valentine M. Moghadam, *Modernizing Women: Gender and Social Change in the Middle East.*2nd ed. (Boulder: Lynne Rienner, 2003) and Moghadam, "Women's Economic Participation in the Middle East: What Difference has the Neoliberal Policy Turn Made?" *Journal of Middle East Women's Studies* 1, no. 1 (2004): 110–46.

[17] Mounira M. Charrad, *States and Women's Rights: The Making of Postcolonial Tunisia, Algeria, and Morocco* (Berkeley: University of California Press, 2001).

achieve their own desired ends. Such scholars, in emphasizing women's capacity to act as agents, also stress the great heterogeneity in the sociopolitical and legal circumstances that Islam underlies, implying again that Islam itself is not the culprit in women's subordination throughout the Muslim world.

The other camp includes scholar-activists, sometimes criticized as "Westoxified," who offer more negative accounts of women's current status and opportunities in Islamic societies.[18] Scholars in this camp, for example, Haideh Moghissi and Hammed Shahidian, acknowledge that Western observers, while blind to the West's own patriarchal shortcomings, have always had ulterior motives for focusing on, and, indeed, sensationalizing, the ill-treatment of women in Muslim societies.[19] At the same time, these scholar-activists are more unqualified in their condemnation of misogyny in the name of Islam, arguing that defensiveness about women's conditions under Islam lapses into dangerous apologetics. For this negative camp, Islam as it has actually developed is indeed a key determinant of women's exceptionally low status in Islamic societies. For them, leaning over backwards to be "culturally sensitive" and to absolve Islam of blame for women's subordination is a dangerous stance that ultimately lends support to, or at least does not counter, the forces of resurgent religion that aim to deepen control over women. Although it might be valid to argue, as the positive camp does, that the sacred texts of Islam *can* be read in non-patriarchal ways, any such "rereadings" carry no real authority. Moreover, the very effort to read or "reread" sacred texts at all in arguing for the betterment of women's status affirms the relevance of Islam to the "woman questions," thereby playing into the hands of religious forces that seek to block the path to separation of religion and state. From the point of view of this negative camp, women's interests are best pursued in secular terms and in the name of combating universal human rights violations.

Uneven Representation of Different Regions, Nations, and Classes

In addition to the tension between interpretive camps, another feature to keep in mind in regard to the scholarship on women and Islam is that it is highly uneven in coverage. The scholarly literature on women in Islamic societies is uneven in the amount of attention that it devotes to different regions, nations, and social classes. Demonstrating what some call

---

[18] The term "Westoxified" translates a pejorative Iranian term.
[19] Haideh Moghissi, *Feminism and Islamic Fundamentalism: The Limits of Postmodern Analysis* (London: Zed Books, 1999), and Hammed Shahidian, *Women in Iran: Gender Politics in the Islamic Republic* (Westport, CT: Greenwood Press, 2003).

"selection bias," studies cluster on particular topics for a variety of reasons and in ways that influence the overall understanding about women. The most notable clustering is simply the predominance of coverage of the mostly Arab Islamic lands of the Middle East and North Africa (MENA). In addition to this disproportionate focus on MENA, studies about gender and Muslim communities in other regions are highly influenced by research on the Arab world, despite the fact that Arab Muslims constitute only about 15 percent of the world's Muslims. The largest single Muslim nation is Indonesia, a nation of about 182 million people in Southeast Asia, the major region that is least covered in the scholarly literature about women. After Indonesia, the next three largest Muslim populations, each exceeding 100 million people, are in the South Asian nations of Pakistan, Bangladesh, and predominantly Hindu India. Despite this, MENA is more thoroughly covered than is South Asia, and the two regions—the "core" Islamic lands of MENA and South Asia—together receive disproportionate treatment compared to Southeast Asia or post-Soviet, Muslim-majority Central Asian countries.

This differential weighting of research by regions affects the understanding of women in Islam, in part because Islam developed differently in different regions. In Southeast Asia, for example, Islam encountered well-established local belief systems that differed markedly from those native to the Middle East and that never entirely disappeared after the acceptance of Islam.[20] This blend yielded a syncretic Southeast Asianized Islam that supports a different and less inegalitarian gender system in such places as Aceh, Sumatra, and elsewhere in Asia, systems that run somewhat against the grain of conventional assumptions regarding Muslim women.[21]

Apart from the clustering of work along regional lines, other clusters are evident in the scholarship. One such notable clustering reflects the influence and special preoccupations of the WID/GAD strand of policy-oriented literature, namely, the clustering on Bangladeshi, specifically, rural women. Bangladesh draws the interest of economically oriented researchers, because the country is a poster child for innovative development efforts targeting women, as well as an exemplar of rapid, state-led socioeconomic change. The best-known experiments in such targeted efforts, the microfinance programs of such NGO-led financial institutions as the Grameen Bank, have become renowned and much-studied for the excellent repayment

---

[20] Anthony Reid, *Southeast Asia in the Age of Commerce 1450–1680*, Vol. 2: *Expansion and Crisis* (New Haven: Yale University Press, 1993), 132–201.
[21] Jacqueline Aquino Siapno, *Gender, Islam, Nationalism, and the State in Aceh: The Paradox of Power, Co-optation, and Resistance* (London: Curzon Routledge, 2002).

performance of their predominantly female borrowers.[22] Evaluating the programs as a model for other underdeveloped countries, development specialists have addressed such narrow questions as the loan use pattern of the women and the loan's immediate economic benefits, and broader questions concerning the loans' impact on women's economic and social empowerment and gender relations. Related studies since the 1970s—mainly intensive field-based works by anthropologists—also analyze the impact of women's entry into wage employment on the freedom of movement of women workers and the perception of their own changed status, as well as on the backlash to the empowerment of women from conservative and fundamentalist segments of society.[23]

Besides such WID/GAD-inspired clusters of work on economically interesting nation-states, other notable clusters focus on women in conflict and crisis situations of particular interest to the West.[24] The most notable clustering of studies deals with Palestinian women, but this focus on women in crisis situations, with relative neglect of women in normal times, has been seen elsewhere, for instance, in Lebanon, Algeria, Iran, Chechnya, or to take a cluster of historical scholarship, the time of partition in India and Pakistan.[25]

---

[22] For a discussion of development interventions and women in Bangladesh, see Naila Kabeer, *"We Don't Do Credit: Nijera Kori Social Mobilisation and the Collective Capabilities of the Poor in Rural Bangladesh* (Dhaka: Nijera Kori, 2002).

[23] For a representative study on Bangladeshi women and such wider economic issues, see Naila Kabeer, *The Power to Choose: Bangladeshi Women and Labour Market Decisions in London and Dhaka* (London: VERSO, 2000). Kabeer, a development economist who researches gender and development issues for government and multilateral agencies and NGOs, examines the lives and labor market behavior of two groups of female Bangladeshi garment workers, women in London and women in Dhaka, Bangladesh. The labor market decisions of the groups run against expectations in that the women in Bangladesh, a poor, conservative Muslim country with a tradition of female seclusion, have entered factories and become a prominent part of the industrial labor force, while in Britain, female Bangladeshi garment workers are largely concentrated in home-based piecework. Using interview methodology, Kabeer draws on the personal testimonies of women in each group to compare how their labor force decisions were made and the impact the decisions had on their lives.

[24] On conflict leading to violence and, specifically, terrorism, see Karla Cunningham, "Cross-Regional Trends in Female Terrorism," *Studies in Conflict & Terrorism* 26, 3 (2003), 171–96.

[25] Significant recent studies on women and the Palestinian/Israeli conflict include:
- Simona Sharoni, *Gender and the Israeli-Palestinian Conflict: The Politics of Women's Resistance* (Syracuse, NY: Syracuse University Press 1995). Essential reading, Sharoni's book examines women's movements among Israelis and Palestinians and discusses their interactions.
- See also Nahla Abdo and Ronit Lentin, eds., *Women and the Politics of Military Confrontation: Palestinian and Israeli Gendered Narratives of Dislocation* (New York: Berghahn Books, 2002).
- Nadera Shalhoub-Kevorkian, "Liberating Voices: The Political Implications of Palestinian Mothers Narrating Their Loss," *Women's Studies International Forum* 26, no. 5 (2003): 391–407 <http://womens-studies.syr.edu/Womens-Studies/CourseReader/OnlineReader/EGMethfemPalestinemoth.pdf>

Recent studies on women and other conflicts include:
- On Lebanon's civil war (1975-90) and women, Lamia Rustum Shehadeh, ed., *Women and War in Lebanon* (Gainesville, FL: University Press of Florida, 1999).
- On Algeria's civil conflict as of 1990, Khalida Messaoudi, *Unbowed: An Algerian Woman Confronts Islamic Fundamentalism: Interviews with Elizabeth Schemla*, trans., Anne C. Vila (Philadelphia, PA:

The strong representation of Iran in the scholarly literature reflects a further factor that often accounts for the clustering of studies on a given area, namely, a concentration of highly educated women from the area. Iran is a focus of much study thanks to many ex-patriate social scientists, including many women now living in the West who managed to gain an education prior to the Khomeini revolution. Egypt has a similarly strong contingent of social scientists interested in gender, including women, thanks to a combination of well-established venues for Western-influenced social science, such as American University, Cairo, and a many decades-long history of women's activism for the dual goals of national and women's advancement.

Sudan has drawn a great deal of attention in studies of women, because it is the epicenter of a combined public health and human rights issue, namely, female genital mutilation. Numerous early studies, fueled by international concerns, addressed the practice and the problems it poses for women.[26] Later studies have taken up the question of how and whether interventions, seen as Western-driven, have hardened resistance to change.[27]

Assessing Women's Status: Categories of Data, Categories of Scholarly Work

Whatever drives the development of particular clusters of research, or variations in the coverage devoted to given regions and nations, the research on Muslim women is partly a function of what data and research tools the larger research community has generated and makes available. Within each of the major topic areas in the research, studies about Muslim women rely upon, and combine in varying proportions, different types of primary data, the generation of which has been in many cases a recent phenomenon.

The Production of Data and Research Tools

Primary statistical data, in particular—an ingredient of much social scientific work on women—were hard to come by prior to the first U.N Decade for Women (1976-1985). Until then, in many sectors of development, there was no commitment to look specifically at women's issues and gender differences and no resource allocation to develop data separately for males and

---

University of Pennsylvania Press, 1998), and Leila Hessini, *Living on a Fault Line: Political Violence Against Women in Algeria* (New York: Population Council, UNIFEM/AFWIC, 1996), and *From Uncivil War to Civil Peace: Algerian Women's Voices* (New York: Population Council, UNIFEM/AFWIC, 1998).
[26] A valuable recent study of the topic is Ellen Gruenbaum, *The Female Circumcision Controversy: An Anthropological Perspective* (Philadelphia: University of Pennsylvania Press, 2001).
[27] See, especially, Sondra Hale, *Gender Politics in Sudan: Islamism, Socialism, and the State* (Boulder: Westview Press, 1998).

females. After the mid-1970s, sex-disaggregated data became a higher priority and the paucity of such information saw gradual, albeit still spotty, improvement. Social indicators such as literacy rate, school enrollment, employment, health, access to nutrition, and the death rate of children were increasingly available not just as averages, but also broken down by sex. Major sources of such information—macro level statistics about women and statistical compilations—are the international organizations, for example, the United Nations system, with the databases of the U.N. Educational, Scientific, and Cultural Organization (UNESCO) and the U.N.'s *World's Women: Trends and Statistics 2000*; the World Bank, with its population databases and GenderStats, a global electronic database of gender statistics and indicators;[28] and the International Labor Organization, with the ILO database *Estimates and Projections of the Economically Active Population, 1950–2010*.[29] Additional sources within the U.N. system include several units of the Statistics Division and the United Nations' Development Program's Time Use Surveys.[30] The United Nations also produces WISTAT, a compilation on CD-ROM of currently available international statistics on the situation of women for 212 countries.[31]

Such statistical sources provide baseline data on the situation and characteristics of women worldwide upon which other studies and cross-national and cross-regional comparisons can be based. The international organizations themselves regularly develop reports, building their analyses on their own and other improving sources of sex-disaggregated data. Notable United Nations reports pertinent to gender worldwide include the annual Human Development Reports, most notably the 1995 and 2004 issues.[32] United Nations reports specifically on the Middle East include an annual series of Arab Human Development Reports, which is a collaboration of the United Nations Development Programme (UNDP) and the Arab Fund for

---

[28] For GenderStats, see <http://devdata.worldbank. org/genderstats/home.asp>

[29] International Labor Organization, *Estimates and Projections of the Economically Active Population, 1950–2010.* <http://www.ilo.org/public/english/bureau/stat/child/actrep/ecacpop.htm>

[30] For U.N. statistics, see
- United Nations, Statistics Division, Demographic and Social Statistics, <http://unstats.un.org/unsd/demographic/default.htm>
- United Nations, Statistics Division. Statistics and Indicators on Women and Men. <http://unstats.un.org/unsd/demographic/products/indwm/table5clx.htm>
- United Nations Development Program (UNDP), Time Use Surveys, <http://unstats.un.org/unsd/methods/timeuse/tusresource.htm>

[31] WISTAT, the *Women's Indicators and Statistics Database*, Reference CD-ROM, Haggard 2.

[32] See, from the United Nations Development Program (UNDP),
- *Human Development Report. Gender and Human Development*, 1995. <http://hdr.undp.org/reports/global/1995/en/>
- United Nations Office of the UN Special Co-ordinator (UNSCO), *Human Development Report. Cultural Liberty in Today's Diverse World*, 2004. <http://hdr.undp.org/reports/global/2004/>

Economic and Social Development. The first regional Human Development Report (HDR) for the Arab States, published in 2002, focuses on the 22 member states of the Arab League, from Maghreb to the Gulf.[33] Examining progress in human development in the last three decades, the report credits the countries with significant strides in several areas, while singling out shortcomings in the areas of women's empowerment, freedom, and knowledge. Since the 2002 report, the series has included 2003 and 2004 reports and will include a 2005 report focused on women's issues. Other reports from within the U.N system stem from the U.N. Development Fund for Women (UNIFEM), whose Arab States Regional Office, for example, sponsors research in its Arab Women Connect project.[34] The project, part of a Women in Development Information Facilitation Initiative, disseminates through its Web site reports and statistics collected from women's organization in cooperating countries. In addition, the United Nations has produced special reports that are pertinent to the conditions of Muslim women, for example, the economic impact of mobility restrictions on Palestinians and gender and energy provision in Bangladesh.[35]

The World Bank is also a major source not only of internationally comparable statistical and economic data, but also of summary reports both for women worldwide and for specific regions. An important 2004 World Bank report pertinent specifically to women in the Middle East argues that women's increased participation in the public sphere is critical to the region's development.[36] The World Bank also produces (alone or in partnership with governments, civil society, and other development agencies) country gender assessments, for example, a 2004 report on Egypt and a 2005 report on Jordan, as well as research on a variety of specific gender issues related to development, such as girl's education in Bangladesh, poverty in Morocco, social protection and employment in the Middle East, and social safety nets worldwide.[37]

---

[33] *Arab Human Development Report 2002: Creating Opportunities for Future Generations*, <http://www.rbas.undp.org/ahdr.cfm>

[34] Arab States Regional Office (ASRO) launched the Arab/English Arab Women Connect (AWC) Web site in 2000. Partners include women's groups in Egypt, Jordan, Lebanon, Palestine, Syria, Yemen, UAE, and Qatar.

[35] The Impact of Closure and Other Mobility Restrictions on Palestinian Productive Activities, October 2002. <www.un.org/news/dh/mideast/econ-reportfinal.pdf>. United Nations Development Programme (UNDP) and World Bank, *Integrating Gender in Energy Provision: Case Study of Bangladesh*, 2004.

[36] *Gender and Development in the Middle East and North Africa: Women in the Public Sphere* (Washington, DC: World Bank, 2004). An extensive list of World Bank documents, Web sites, and other resources addressing gender issues is available at: <http://www.worldbank.org/gender>

[37] See the following World Bank reports:
- *Egypt: Gender Assessment Report*, 2004.
- *The Economic Advancement of Women in Jordan: A Country Gender Assessment*, May 2005,
- *Access to Education for the Poor and Girls: Education Achievements in Bangladesh* (Washington, DC: World Bank, 2004).

In compiling such reports and basic data, the major international organizations draw in their turn upon the statistical capacities of national governments, whether advanced nations, which contribute to the collection of internationally comparable large-scale data, or developing and aid-recipient nations, whose ministries increasingly collect sex-disaggregated data when assessing their own development efforts. One such contribution by an advanced nation is a United States government, specifically Social Security Administration (SSA), source pertinent to women worldwide, on social security programs around the world.[38] Among developing nations, Pakistan provides a typical example in its efforts to improve its collection of national gender statistics and gender indices. Continuing the colonial government's practice of conducting the decadal census, the current government operates through its official statistical organizations to collect vital statistics on marriage, divorce, and birth rates and through ministries of education, labor, and social affairs to produce annual reports. As the government increasingly viewed women's well-being as relevant to development, it underwrote the study of women to track progress. In 1985, the government appointed a commission on the status of women, which issued its findings as a report.[39] Pakistan's national contributions, like such contributions elsewhere, partly relied in turn on the work of women-centered NGOs. NGOs associated with development interventions regularly generate data and analyses, as well as field-based studies via their independent research units. Such NGOs are often the source and impetus for data collection on sensitive subjects, such as violence against women and women's disadvantage in access to resources, such as property.

As the combined efforts of international organizations, national governments, and NGOs provide better sources of sex-disaggregated data, they contribute to improvements in the ability to assess the status of women cross-regionally.

- *Claiming the Future: Choosing Prosperity in the Middle East and North Africa* (Washington, DC: World Bank, 1995).
- *Moroccan Poverty Report* (Washington, DC: World Bank, 2001).
- *Reducing Vulnerability and Increasing Opportunity: A Strategy for Social Protection in Middle East and North Africa* (Washington, DC: World Bank, 2002).
- *Social Safety Nets* <http://www1.worldbank.org/sp/safetynets/Keyconcepts%20asp>
- *Unlocking the Employment Potential in the Middle East and North Africa: Toward a New Social Contract* (Washington, DC: World Bank, 2004).

[38] *Social Security Programs Throughout the World*, 1999. <http://www.ssa.gov/policy/docs/progdesc/ssptw/1999/#toc>

[39] Government of Pakistan, *Report of the Pakistan Commission on the Status of Women* (Islamabad: Pakistan Commission on the Status of Women, 1989).

Combining Indicators to Measure the Well-being of Women

A major step in the global research community's capacity to analyze women's condition and gender-based inequality also has been the development of several composite measures of female well-being. These measures debuted with the issuance of the 1995 United Nations Development Program (UNDP) Human Development Report. Earlier versions of this annual report, which was first issued in 1990, used a single aggregate measure, the Human Development Index (HDI), to capture the average national level of human development and well-being across nations. The HDI ranks countries by combining a number of socioeconomic indicators: literacy, educational attainment, and per capita income. The HDI, as a composite measurement, expresses a critique of narrow development ideology, which measures development simply in terms of growth and production (as measured by GNP/GDP).[40] However, the HDI is not designed to register gender-based differences in access to economic resources and power. The two new composite measures introduced with the 1995 Human Development Report remedied this omission. The first, the Gender Development Index (GDI), measures the same variables as the HDI, but also adjusts the achievements of the various countries for gender disparities in life expectancy, in educational attainment, and in gross national product (GNP) per capita.[41] The second aggregate index, the Gender Empowerment Measure (GEM), assesses women's ability to participate actively in economic and political life by combining measures of women's representation in the highest levels of government (parliaments), women's share of managerial and professional positions, and female participation in the active labor force. Taken together, the two measures of well-being represent an advance in allowing international comparisons of women's access relative to men's to resources and power. The measures have their limitations, including the fact that, like other socioeconomic indicators, they deal in averages that can mask

---

[40] Over the last two decades, numerous alternatives to GDP/GNP have been proposed for measuring economic development. For a survey on a number of these alternatives, including HDI, see Richard W. England and Jonathan M. Harris, "Alternatives to Gross National Product: A Critical Survey," in Frank Ackerman, David Kiron, Neva Goodwin, Jonathan Harris, and Kevin P. Gallagher, eds., *Human Well-Being and Economic Goals* (Washington, DC:.Island Press, 1998). Many early efforts to devise GNP/GDP alternatives built upon the pioneering work of William Nordhaus and James Tobin, who first calculated a Measure of Economic Welfare in 1972, taking account of such factors as unpaid household labor and "urban disamenities." As England and Harris indicate, subsequent substitute measures have sought to varying degrees to address the following issues:
- the need to distinguish between "goods" and "bads",
- the need to account for asset depreciation in both manufactured and natural assets,
- the need to divide output between consumption and capital accumulation,
- the need to take account of non-marketed goods and services, and
- the need to take account of the welfare implications of various forms of social inequality.

differences in women's status by class.[42] Moreover, the measures are only as good as data they rely upon. Not all U.N. member countries have sufficient data available to calculate the indices. Coverage of the GDI is limited to 143 countries, GEM to 70 countries. GEM estimates, in particular, are available for only a limited number of Arab Muslim countries.

Improving Data

Efforts to improve further the generation of data in Muslim societies—efforts often involving the collaboration of international organizations—are ongoing. Recent examples of such efforts include the Gender Equality Measured through Statistics project (GEMS), a project initiated by the United Nations Fund For Women (UNIFEM), Arab States Regional Office in partnership with departments of statistics and civic organizations working on women's advancement in Egypt, Jordan, and Syria. The GEMS initiative aims to strengthen the countries' statistical monitoring systems, helping them measure progress in fulfilling their national and international commitments to further gender equality. The initiative also aims at a common framework of best statistical practices for Arab countries.[43] Other initiatives to improve gender indicators and statistics include workshops held in United Arab Emirates and Beirut in 2003. These workshops were supported by the United Nations Economic and Social Commission for Western Asia (ESCWA), UNIFEM, Center of Arab Women for Training and Research (CAWTAR), and UNFPA.

The social scientists that work on Muslim women are mindful of the state of available sex-disaggregated data, and frequently offer observations on both their improvement and limitations. Jennifer Olmsted, for instance—who is among the few practitioners of conventional economics studying Muslim women—discusses problems of using aggregate statistics, faulting the GDI and GEM for their inability to capture class inequities along with gender inequities.[44] She also finds the issue of relative workloads between men and women to be a crucial gender equity issue that escapes most current statistical measures. She sees promise in using time-use survey data or measurements of leisure among gender equality indicators, because time-use data

---

[41] Starting with a perfect score of one, the GDI formula decreases a country's score as its disparity between men and women increases.

[42] The measures may also fail to provide a consistent story, in that women in a given country may appear well off using one measure and far worse of using the other.

[43] UNIFEM, *Progress of Arab Women, 65.*

[44] Jennifer C. Olmsted, "Is Paid Work The (Only) Answer? Neoliberalism, Arab Women's Well-Being, and the Social Contract," *Journal of Middle East Women's Studies* 1, no. 2 (Spring 2005): 112–41.

can capture whether women's increased paid work is accompanied by a decrease in women's unpaid workload or simply results, because of gender norms, in a "double burden" of work for women. The political economists Valentine Moghadam and Nabil Khoury discuss similar issues of data deficiencies and shortcomings of statistical indicators throughout their work. Moghadam compares the availability of sex-disaggregated data in a number of Middle Eastern countries, finding inconsistent definitions of work and spotty collection in many, shifting categorizations in Iran, and relatively good collection in Tunisia.[45] Moghadam and Khoury, in a book published for the United Nations University's World Institute for Development Economics Research, note the dearth of detailed studies on women and economic development in Arab countries and argue that improved sex-disaggregated statistical information is essential for assessing the realistic economic contribution of Arab women to the region's development. Short of such a correct assessment, they argue, the formulation of adequate development policies is unlikely.[46]

Specialized and Microstudies

The growth and availability of primary statistics, statistical compilations, and indicators are important in the study of Muslim women, because such basic information serves as the foundation and/or starting point for social scientific effort that goes beyond large-scale aggregate statistical work. Most of the published empirical work on Muslim women consists of article-length studies that focus on one or several countries and a limited range of issues within a particular discipline's purview. Book-length works are generally multi-authored edited collections of articles, typically featuring introductory material that sets up a theme, followed by a number of "case studies." Book-length, single-authored studies, or monographs, sustained and thematic, are still exceptional.

The monographs that do appear are predominantly closely focused ethnographic, in-depth studies of particular communities, rural and non-elite as well as urban and middle- or upper class. Often focusing on household survival and livelihood strategies, such monographs rely on evidence derived from field research and methods favored by anthropologists: participant observation supplemented with oral histories, open-ended interviews, and sometimes

---

[45] Valentine M. Moghadam, "Women's Economic Participation in the Middle East: What Difference has the Neoliberal Policy Turn Made?" *Journal of Middle East Women's Studies* 1, no. 1 (2004): 110–46.

[46] Nabil F. Khoury and Valentine M. Moghadam, eds., *Gender and Development in the Arab World: Women's Economic Participation: Patterns and Policies* (Tokyo: Zed Books and United Nations University Press, 1995).

questionnaires.[47] In such monographs, the material from field research is generally supplemented with narrative accounts of pertinent historical background and developments in policy. Monographic studies of this type include, for example, Homa Hoodfar's ethnography on households in Cairo, which uses participant observation and questionnaires to examine the daily life of a sample of low income Arab Muslim families.[48] A less common type of monograph—a type often produced by researchers in South Asia—is a statistics-laden description of a highly local community. In addition to relying on government statistics at various levels of generality, the researcher questions a sample of respondents for a detailed quantitative breakdown on numerous aspects of life, e.g., marital status (how many currently married, how many widowed), employment status (how many in what types of work), diseases, delivery practices, household expenditures, and decision-making in the household. A representative Indian study of this descriptive type is an examination by sociologist P.V.L. Ramana of women in a Muslim slum in India.[49]

In the corpus of article-length studies on Muslim women, researchers avail themselves directly of field research, if at all, on a more modest scale. Articles often offer their analyses using non-field-based materials such as selected published statistics, pertinent published laws and policy pronouncements, narrative accounts of court cases as gleaned from court transcripts, narratives of events, analyses of media, and secondary accounts of other's field-based surveys, public opinion polls, or interviews and personal testimony. Studies that incorporate direct field-based material typically use it as a small, albeit key, piece of a larger discussion. For instance, in addressing why women are drawn to Islamist movements despite their apparent sexism, Jodi Nachtwey and Mark Tessler cite evidence from the public opinion research they conducted with a sample of women.[50] (As discussed below, the evidence suggests that women are drawn to such movements for essentially the same reasons as are men.) Occasionally articles that incorporate evidence from field-based research deploy it for formal theory- or hypothesis testing that involves the use of a control group. Such work is typically associated with public health

---

[47] For a series of articles by Arab women who have done anthropological work in the Middle East through the 1980s see Soraya Altorki and C. F. El-Solh, *Arab Women in the Field. Studying Your Own Society* (Syracuse, NY: Syracuse University Press, 1988).

[48] Homa Hoodfar, *Between Marriage and the Market: Intimate Politics and Survival in Cairo* (Berkeley: University of California Press, 1997).

[49] P.V.L. Ramana, *Women in Slums: A Study of Women in a Muslim Slum of Visakhapatnam* (New Delhi: Serials Publications, 2002).

[50] Jodi Nachtwey and Mark Tessler, "Explaining Women's Support for Political Islam: Contributions from Feminist Theory," 48–69, in Mark Tessler, with Jodi Nachtwey and Anna Banda, eds., *Area Studies and Social Science: Strategies for Understanding Middle East Politics* (Bloomington: Indiana University Press, 1999).

interventions, but goes beyond narrow health questions to address relevant social questions. A representative study of this type examines family planning service provision in Bangladesh.[51] These authors use the occasion of service provision to consider how particular modes of provision affect women's empowerment. They test the hypothesis that the country's famous "doorstep services," in which women receive family planning services at home, reinforce the customs of patriarchy and *purdah* (female seclusion) by sustaining the dependency and isolation of women. The authors compare the scores of groups of women on two standardized women's status surveys instruments, and conclude that the hypothesis cannot be supported. Whatever the mode of service delivery, the mere fact of receiving contraceptive services can positively affect women's status.

Consolidation of Knowledge about Women in Islamic Societies

Although most empirical work on Muslim women still consists of modest-scale studies, field-based or otherwise, the scholarly corpus on women in Islamic cultures is currently sufficiently mature to have brought forth a number of projects of consolidation. The most ambitious and massive is the *Encyclopedia of Women and Islamic Cultures*.[52] Under the general editorship of Suad Joseph, the *Encyclopedia* is projected to consist of five large volumes, the first of which, subtitled *Methodologies, Paradigms, and Sources*, was published in 2003. Entries in the first volume are organized in accordance with several concepts, including period, region, nation-state, and discipline. The volume is organized in two sections. The authors of the articles in the first section cover diverse regions, with entries on historical periods from the sixth century in the Middle East, just before the rise of Islam there, and just prior to the introduction of Islam in other regions, to the present. The second section consists of disciplinary entries, spanning the major disciplines as well as interdisciplinary fields, such as women's studies/gender studies, Islamic studies, and legal studies, and also conceptual/methodological fields such as "Orientalism" and "oral history." The volume also contains bibliographies for each entry and a 200-page comprehensive bibliography organized by country and subject areas.

In addition to the *Encyclopedia*, there are several single-discipline overviews and retrospective surveys of the state of the discipline's research on women in Islamic cultures.

---

[51] James F. Phillips and Mian Bazle Hossain, *The Impact of Family Planning Household Service Delivery on Women's Status in Bangladesh*, no. 118, 1998. <http://www.popcouncil.org/pdfs/wp/118.pdf>
[52] Suad Joseph, et al, ed., *Encyclopedia of Women and Islamic Cultures: Methodologies, Paradigms, and Sources*, Vol. I (Leiden, Netherlands: Brill, 2003).

Although far more modest than the *Encyclopedia*, these too bespeak a certain maturity of the research area. Examples of such overviews in the field of history include two articles by Nikki Keddie, "The Study of Muslim Women in the Middle East: Achievements and Remaining Problems," and "Women in the Limelight: Some Recent Books on Middle Eastern Women's History."[53]

IV. DIMENSIONS OF WOMEN'S STATUS AND BODIES OF RESEARCH

The expanding corpus of research on women addresses itself to all of the major dimensions or arenas of women's lives. With regard to most of these dimensions—the legal system, health, family, economics, and politics—the matters under discussion are concrete and involve female disadvantage that is measurable in terms of real gender gaps in opportunities and access to resources. One dimension that is a major topic in the literature, however, is non-material in nature, namely, cultural understandings about appropriate womanhood, particularly as these understandings are embodied and conveyed in religion.

Sex-Role Ideologies and Feminist Discourses: Examining Sacred Texts and Contexts

A significant percentage of scholars who focus on women in the Muslim world, particularly women scholars of Muslim background or Islamic faith, devote at least some of their scholarly energies to grappling with cultural ideas or "discourses" about appropriate female roles and conduct and, more specifically, with what Leila Ahmed calls "the core discourses of Islam," the Qur'an, (divine revelation), the Sunna (deeds and sayings of the prophet Muhammed), the Hadith (interpretive moral codes based on sayings of the prophet), and other sacred writings.[54] Among the numerous scholars who are known for offering sustained analysis of the Qur'anic formulations of gender are Leila Ahmed, Margot Badran, Asma Barlas, Fatima Mernissi, Riffat Hassan, Ziba Mir Hosseini, Barbara Stowasser, and Amina Wadud.[55]

---

[53] Nikki Keddie, "The Study of Muslim Women in the Middle East: Achievements and Remaining Problems," in *Harvard Middle Eastern and Islamic Review* 6 (2000): 26–52; and Keddie, "Women in the Limelight: Some Recent Books on Middle Eastern Women's History," in *International Journal of Middle East Studies* 34, no. 3 (2002): 553–73.

[54] Leila Ahmed, *Women and Gender in Islam: Historical Roots of a Modern Debate* (New Haven: Yale University Press, 1992).

[55] Key titles of and on such exegesis include:

- Leila Ahmed, *Women and Gender in Islam: Historical Roots of a Modern Debate* (New Haven: Yale University Press, 1992).

In offering such analyses of Islam's sacred writings, the scholars subject to scrutiny the scriptural foundations customarily cited to justify restrictions on women's roles and autonomy in the family and society. These scholars avoid questioning the sacrality of the scriptures, some out of personal belief and some out of conviction as to the strategic value of deploying a religious idiom to counter patriarchal religious discourse.[56] They rehearse and criticize the justifications that are used by conservatives and radical Muslims to restrict women's rights. Showing that the justifications lack sufficient basis in Islamic texts, the scholars highlight textual bases for alternatives to the dominantly male interpretations.

In thus addressing Islam as a religious discourse, the scholars do not necessarily commit to the idea that ideology or religious constructs constitute primary determinants of women's roles and material circumstances. The focus on Islam does not imply a privileging of Islam as an explanatory category. The Moroccan sociologist Fatima Mernissi, for example, is a pioneer in alternative women-centered exegesis, but at the same time, true to her training as a sociologist, de-emphasizes the degree to which the Qur'an and even Islamic jurisprudence trumps other factors, such as socioeconomic realities and change, as the main determinants of female status in Muslim lands.

Not privileging "Islam" or ideology in general as an ultimate determinant, the scholars affirm only that it is worthwhile to undermine sexist discourse, inasmuch as such discourse plays a legitimizing role in women's second-class status. Religion is not the sole embodiment and conveyor of patriarchal ideology in Muslim or any other societies. However, Islamic modes of

---

- Margot Badran and Miriam Cooke, eds. *Opening the Gates: An Anthology of Arab Feminist Writing*, 2nd ed. (Bloomington: Indiana University Press, 2004).
- Asma Barlas, *Believing Women in Islam: Unreading Patriarchal Interpretations of the Qur'an* (Austin: University of Texas Press, 2002).
- Riffat Hassan, "Equal Before Allah: Woman/Man Equality in the Islamic Tradition', *Harvard Divinity Bulletin 7*, no. 2, (Jan-May 1987).
- Z. Mir-Hosseini, *Islam and Gender: The Religious Debate in Contemporary Iran* (New Haven: Princeton University Press, 1999).
- Fatima Mernissi, *Women and Islam: An Historical and Theological Enquiry*, trans. by Mary Jo Lakeland (Oxford: Blackwell, 1991); and *The Veil and the Male Elite: A Feminist Interpretation of Women's Rights in Islam* (Reading, MA: Addison-Wesley, 1991).
- Barbara Stowasser, "Gender Issues in Contemporary Qur'anic Interpretation," 30–44, in Yvonne Y. Haddad and John L. Esposito, *Islam, Gender, and Social Change*, (New York: Oxford University Press, 1998); and *Women in the Qur'an, Traditions, and Interpretation*.
- Amina Wadud, *Qur'an and Woman: Reading the Sacred Text from a Woman's Perspective* (NewYork: Oxford University Press, 1999).

[56] Among those who engage in scriptural exegesis to retrieve its emancipatory message, some of the believers have been categorized as Islamic feminists. The term "Islamic feminist" refers to scholar and activists who advocate women's rights within an Islamic framework. For further discussion see the section "Women in Muslim States and Politics."

reasoning and argumentation play a prominent and explicit justificatory role, and, some argue, even an unusually prominent role, as religious discourse goes.[57] Moreover, Islamic symbols and discourse have gained new legitimacy with the recent resurgence of conservative Islam.[58] Many of the scholars explicitly indicate that they take this task of countering patriarchal readings of Islam to be particularly urgent in view of this religious resurgence.

In taking on patriarchal discourse, scholars have adopted various stances and strategies. The main strategies are to undertake actual engagement with the texts, i.e., to adopt the techniques of textual exegesis more characteristic of theological than of social scientific argument. The other main strategy is to show that the history of such interpretive engagement with the sacred writings has yielded profound variations in interpretation, so that, in effect, it is wrong-headed to think in terms of a single monolithic "Islam." In general, scholars use both strategies in combination.

The conclusion from textual analysis is generally either that the Qur'an's revelation is inherently ethical and egalitarian in spirit or that the Qur'an is an open text and its teachings are, as Moghadam put it, inherently "no more or less patriarchal than other major religions, especially Hinduism and the other two Abrahamic religions, Judaism and Christianity, all of which share the view of woman as wife and mother."[59] In the first view, it is patriarchal readings of the Qur'an and the *fiqh* (rules of jurisprudence), as well as the structure of religious and sexual power in Muslim societies, rather than "Islam," that discriminate against women. The Qur'an has an intrinsic meaning that supports a gender egalitarian reading. In the second view, Islam's sacred texts are bound up with their time and place and, therefore, like Christian texts, harbor a dual tradition. The "texts themselves" embody egalitarian principles whereby women and men have moral equality, along with misogynist conceptions that cite the differences between men

---

[57] On this particular prominence, see William R. Darrow, "Marxism and Religion: Islam," in Charles Wei-hsun Fu and Gerhard E. Spiegler, eds., *Movements and Issues in World Religions: A Sourcebook and Analysis of Developments Since 1945* (Westport, Conn.: Greenwood Press, 1987). As Darrow sees the situation, it is in terms of Islam and/or in Islamic terms that political and social issues are addressed by most inhabitants of the contemporary Islamic world. That others assent to this view is suggested by the large proportion of work on women in Islam that centers on religious discourses. This importance accorded religious inquiry by Muslim scholar-activists distinguishes the body of work from that on non-Muslim, especially Western, societies. While early "second-wave" feminist work—work since the 1970s—on non-Muslim societies took exposing ideologies of female subordination to be a necessary part of understanding the role and status of women, this exposure was not focused so exclusively and persistently on religious discourse. In Muslim contexts, as well as Western, however, work on discourses seems to serve as a "consciousness-raising" stage that fuels subsequent scholarly efforts in various disciplinary arenas to render women's actual experience and particular contributions visible.

[58] Miriam Cooke, *Women Claim Islam: Creating Islamic Feminism Through Literature* (New York: Routledge, 2001), 434.

[59] Moghadam, *Modernizing Women*, 5.

and women as the justification for female subordination to men. For the very reason that the texts harbor this duality, they demand ongoing reinterpretation to disentangle outmoded cultural ideas and practices from the authentic Qur'anic norms and message of revelation.

A proponent of the first view is, for example, Barlas, in her book, *"Believing Women" in Islam: Unreading Patriarchal Interpretations of the Qur'an.* Challenging or "unreading" what she calls "patriarchal exegesis" of the Qur'an, she presents her book as an attempt to "recover the scriptural basis of sexual equality in Islam and thereby to defend Islam" against the claim that it is a religious patriarchy that "professes models of hierarchical relationships and sexual inequality."[60] Mernissi is similarly inclined to offer rereadings that absolve sacred texts of inherent patriarchal ideology. She speaks of "the beautiful Islam of the Prophet Mohammed" who was a "defender of women's dignity and opened Mosques to women on an equal footing with men."[61] Summarizing her forays into demonstrating the compatibility of Mohammed's vision and gender equality, she observes

> One gets a sense of how easy it would be to find data from the religious scriptures and classical history to sustain human rights and women's dignity (if that were the goal of the Muslim states and the political leadership . . .who claim religion as a base).[62]

Ziba Mir-Hosseini, an anthropologist of Iranian background, also offers textual reinterpretations in her book on Islam and gender, which focuses on religious debate in contemporary Iran.[63] Her contribution to the current spate of such rereadings has the distinction of being a transcription of actual dialogues she had with several eminent Islamic *ulema* (clerical scholars) in Iran. She recounts a face-to-face encounter on gender issues

> between adherents of Islamic discourses on gender who are trying to respond to challenges presented by women, and Muslim women like me [Mir-Hosseini], with complex identities, who seek to reconcile their feminism with their faith.[64]

On both sides of the encounter—a clash of different conceptual frameworks and modes of argumentation—a central concern is where authority resides as to the true Qur'anic construction of gender.

---

[60] Asma Barlas, *"Believing Women" in Islam: Unreading Patriarchal Interpretations of the Qur'an* (Austin: University of Texas Press, 2002), 203.
[61] Mernissi, *Women's Rebellion and Islamic Memory* (London: Zed Books, 1996), xii.
[62] Mernissi, *Women's Rebellion*, xii.
[63] Mir-Hosseini, *Islam and Gender: The Religious Debate in Contemporary Iran*.
[64] Mir-Hosseini, 11.

Other scholars, scholars of the second view mentioned, are less easy than Barlas, Mernissi, Mir-Hosseini, and others on Islam's sacred writings, acknowledging that they do offer some scriptural support for male domination. Although more enlightened and gender-egalitarian than the pre-Islamic patriarchal culture in which they arose, they also bear its stamp. This cultural embeddedness of sacred writings only means that they are continuously in need of interpretation to highlight their emancipatory thrust over their remnants of outmoded traditionalism. Such interpretation calls for seeing sacred texts in their historical context and adapting their message to the needs of the age. The scholars with this primary emphasis occupy themselves as much with the processes and history of Qur'anic interpretation as with the texts themselves. In exhaustive detail, they demonstrate that the sacred writings have always been subject to divergent interpretations, notwithstanding strenuous efforts by the interpreters to claim authority for particular readings. A notable example of such inquiry into Islam's interpretive traditions is Leila Ahmed's *Women and Gender in Islam: Historical Roots of a Modern Debate.* Ahmed examines discourses on women and gender in periods of Arab history from ancient (pre-Islamic times in Mesopotamia and the Mediterranean Middle East) to modern periods (and primarily modern Egypt). She stresses the existence of divergent perspectives on gender relations in Islam, while at the same time emphasizing that all strands of "legalistic Islam" were products of societies' dominant groups and the male legal establishment. In such hands, "ethical Islam," with its central values of justice, piety, and equality of all before God, took a back seat to a discourse adapted to the patriarchal mores and social realities of a given period. Mernissi likewise stresses the domination of interpretation by male elites. When asserting that the Qur'an itself does not assign women a subordinate position, she always augments her scriptural exegesis with both historical and sociological observations, often blunt and colorful, about the social interests and misogyny that the hegemonic interpretations of sacred writings reflect. In several books, including *Beyond the Veil: Male-Female Dynamics in a Modern Muslim Society* and *The Veil and the Male Elite: A Feminist Interpretation of Women's Rights in Islam*, she explores in-depth how Qur'anic interpretations and Islamic legal discourse mirror the world views and interests of specific groupings of socially powerful men.[65] Elsewhere, she speaks of the "Petro-Islam" used by present-day Saudi Arabian elites to bolster their political legitimacy. Such Islam draws upon "a rich tradition of misogyny which was heavily revived and technologically backed

---

[65] *Beyond the Veil* (Bloomington, IN: University of Indiana Press, 1987; orig. 1975); *The Veil and the Male Elite.*

(television, state monopoly over school textbooks, etc.)."[66] Mernissi, like Ahmed and others, uses the strategy of "historicizing" and "situating" patriarchal readings of scripture to debunk their claims to authority and to clear the ground for alternatives.

Other exercises in updating Islam and accounts of modern trends in Qur'anic interpretation include works by Barbara Stowasser and Mervat Hatem. In a collection edited by Yvonne Haddad and John L. Esposito, for example, Hatem examines secular and Islamist discourses on modernity and gender, focusing on post-colonial Egypt.[67] In addition to works that offer and describe interpretations, a number of studies address the effect of increased female participation in the processes of interpreting religious discourse. Amel Boubekur discusses female religious professionals in France, Zehra Kamalkami examines female religious practice in Turkey, and Anne Sophie Roald compares feminist reinterpretations of scripture by Muslims and Christians.[68]

Legal Contexts: Women's Legal Position and Rights

Whatever the particular strategy adopted in grappling with Islamic "discourses," a major impetus for the recent plethora of such exercises has been the perceived new threat of widespread legal changes that will be detrimental to women posed by religious revivalism. Almost everywhere in the Muslim world, religion-based law is a component of the legal system, and a major demand of resurgent Islam, whether in Iran, Malaysia, Algeria, Bangladesh, Sudan, Afghanistan, Iraq, Nigeria, or elsewhere, has been revisions in the part of the legal system—the personal status or family laws—whose foundational sources are the Qur'an and Islam's other sacred texts. Addressing religious doctrine thus aims not just at undermining normative cultural notions of gender—patriarchal rationales for women's subordination—but also at challenging aspects of current or proposed women-unfriendly laws of the land. The exegesis of canonical

---

[66] Mernissi, *Women's Rebellion*, xii.

[67] Mervat Hatem, "Secular and Islamist Discourses on Modernity in Egypt and Evolution of the Postcolonial Nation-State," 85–99, in Yvonne Haddad and John L. Esposito, *Islam, Gender, and Social Change*.

[68] See

- Amel Boubekeur, "Female Religious Professionals in France," in *International Institute for the Study of Islam in the Modern World Newsletter*, no.14, 2004. <http://www.isim.nl/files/newsl_14/newsl_14-28.pdf>
- Zehra Kamalkhani, *Women's Islam: Religious Practice among Women in Today's Iran* (London: Kegan Paul International 1998).
- Anne Sophie Roald, " Feminist Reinterpretation of Islamic Sources: Muslim Feminist Theology in the Light of the Christian Tradition of Feminist Thought," in Karin Ask and Marit Tjomsland, eds., *Women and Islamization* (Oxford: Berg, 1998).

texts and the historical study of their further elaboration by Islamic jurisprudence are part and parcel of the academic study of Muslim countries' legal systems, systems that not only embody normative views, but also have "real" consequences for women.

While the study of religious texts and tradition constitute part of legal studies, they are also only a beginning. The body of work on such systems and how they affect women encompasses a number of additional strands. One major strand addresses provisions of the legal systems and the way the systems, often fully codified for the first time in the twentieth century, were put together, incorporating components of both Western-influenced civil laws and religious-based laws. This strand also examines the degree to which the national legal systems in almost all countries have reformed, modifying, and, in rare cases, eliminating their religion-based components. The scholarly corpus that addresses the legal situation of women also includes an innovative strand of mostly anthropological and historical, and some policy-oriented, work on legal practice. Such work focuses not on legal provisions or their reform, but on the ways the provisions actually play out in women's lives. Work in this strand examines institutions of the judicial system and women's experience with them. The work also exploits novel evidential material, including court proceedings, litigant interviews, and *fatwa* (expert legal opinions), to document not only women's disadvantage in the face of discriminatory laws, but also their reasons for bringing cases and their litigant strategies when they do so.

Dual Legal Systems and Family Law Reform: Challenging the Substance of Laws

As they exist today, the legal systems in Islamic societies are almost all dual systems. The most notable exceptions are Turkey and Tunisia, with their purely secular and hence unitary systems.[69] The dual systems are comprised, on the one hand, of a civil code—often Western-inspired—and, on the other hand, a personal status or family law, mainly built upon Sharia law. Analogous to canon law within Christianity, Sharia law consists of legal provisions that rest on interpretations of sacred texts. Sharia jurisprudence, originally uncodified, came to be incorporated as part of most Muslim legal systems as these took shape during the formation of modern Muslim states. The first codification of Sharia law as Islamic Family Law, the Ottoman

---

[69] See Nagat El-Sanabary, "Women in Some Liberal Modernizing Islamic Countries," 515–23, in Nelly P. Stromquist and Karen Monkman, eds., *Women in the Third World: An Encyclopedia of Contemporary Issues* (New York: Garland, 1998).

Law of Family Rights, took place in 1917.[70] Sharia law is generally only one part of a dual system, because it is silent on many matters that pertain to the operation of modern states.[71] Giving little guidance on many commercial matters, for example, Sharia is retained as the part of the legal system that regulates personal status matters: marriages, maintenance, divorces, custody of children, inheritance rights, and the like.

A good deal of scholarly work on the legal situation of Muslim women occupies itself with discussion of the interplay in particular legal systems of different types of law.[72] Although the systems are typically dual, they differ amongst themselves in the degree to which they reflect Western influences and in which countries' influences they reflect. In the course of nation-building, the civil codes of nations incorporated French, Swiss, and Belgian elements, among others. The area of family law, relatively exempt from Western influences because of the availability of an indigenous alternative, is also complicated by the multiple influences. When family laws were codified and modernized across the Muslim world, they drew upon a number of Sunni schools of law (Hanafi, Maliki, Hanbali, Shafii), which differ in the ways in which they structure family relations, and differ as well from Shia law, which has two schools of jurisprudence (Jafari and Zaydi).[73] Moreover, the family laws blend elements from Islamic schools with features of local pre-Islamic or tribal/ethnic customary law, as well as features of Western jurisprudence.[74]

This complicated array of influences yields many variations in the provisions that appear in the legal systems in Muslim countries, and, in particular, in the family or personal status laws.

---

[70] Annelies Moors, "Debating Islamic Family Law: Legal Texts and Social Practices," 141–75, in Margaret L. Meriwether and Judith E. Tucker, eds., *Social History of Women and Gender in the Modern Middle East* (Boulder: Westview Press, 1999), 151.

[71] See John L. Esposito, with Natana J. DeLong-Bas, *Women in Muslim Family Law*, 2nd ed. (Syracuse, NY: Syracuse University Press, 2001, orig., 1982). According to Esposito, commercial, penal, and criminal laws changed dramatically throughout the modern period, while Muslim family law remained relatively unchanged until the early twentieth century.

[72] For an example of such discussions, see the background material on Jordan in Amira El-Azhary Sonbol, *Women of Jordan: Islam, Labor and the Law*. Gender, Culture, and Politics in the Middle East Series (Syracuse, NY: Syracuse University Press, 2003.

[73] Other contemporary schools of law include the Ibadi and Thahiri schools. Islam's 1,400 years of history has witnessed scores of schools of jurisprudence, many progressive and woman-friendly. On the differences among the various contemporary Sunni schools, see Ahmed, 88ff. Ahmed discusses, among other topics, differences among the schools' provisions on marriage guardianship of women, on their options to ask courts for annulment, and on whether adult women may arrange marriages for themselves or requires consent of the guardian.

[74] For general background on the sources and evolution of Islamic law, see Wael B. Hallaq, *The Origins and Evolution of Islamic Law* (Cambridge, U.K.; New York: Cambridge University Press, 2005). Hallaq, an eminent scholar in the field of Islamic law, analyzes how Islam developed its own law from ancient Near Eastern legal cultures, Arabian customary law, and Qur'anic sources. Covering three centuries, the book explores the interplay between law and politics, demonstrating how jurists and ruling elites together allowed Islamic law to become uniquely independent of the "state."

Although there is no fully "typical" system, most of them contain some to many of the provisions and formulations that would make up a "wish list" of conservatives and Islamists. This "wish list"—and to varying degrees, reality—has the following provisions: Religious affiliation is a requirement of citizenship. Although women have the right to own and dispose of property, they inherit less property than men. Women have the right to only half the amount of inheritance that their brothers receive. Male members of the kin group have extensive control over key decisions affecting "their" women's lives. Women are required to obtain permission of father, husband, or other male guardian to marry, seek employment, start a business, or travel. Although the highly formal Islamic marriage contract may or may not require the consent of the wife (depending on the Sunni school relied upon), marriage is largely an agreement between two families rather than two individuals with equal rights and obligations. Marriage gives the husband the right of access to his wife's body, and marital rape is not recognized. Only men have the right to divorce unilaterally and without cause. There is no provision for alimony. Polygamy on the part of a man is allowed. Shia law permits the contracting of temporary marriages for specified periods of time. Women are not granted guardianship of minor children in the case of the father's death. Children acquire citizenship and religious status through their fathers, not their mothers. Muslim women may not marry non-Muslim men. The criminal code provides for acquittal or a reduction of sentence for men who commit "honor" crimes.

The scholarship on women and Muslim legal systems provides ample research by which to gauge the actual fulfillment of this conservative "wish list" in particular countries.[75] A good

---

[75] On countries outside the Middle East, see,
- Ustaz Yoonus Abdullah, *Sharia in Africa* (Ijebu-Ode, Nigeria: Shebiotimo Publications, 1998).
- Azizah Y. Al-Hibri, "Islamic Law and Muslim Women in America," in Marjorie Garber, and Rebecca L. Walkowitz, eds., *One Nation Under God? Religion and American Culture* (New York: Routledge, 1999).
- Amer M. Bara-Acal, and Abdulmajid J. Astih, *Muslim Law on Personal Status in the Phillipines* (Quezon City, Phillipines: Central Professional Books, 1998).
- Firoz Cachalia, *The Future of Muslim Family Law in South Africa* (London: Centre for Applied Legal Studies and Johannesburg, University of the Witwatersrand. South African Constitutional Studies Centre, Institute of Commonwealth Studies, 1991).
- Sharifa Zaleha Syed Hassan, and Sven Cedrroth,. *Managing Marital Disputes in Malaysia: Islamic Mediators and Conflict Resolution in the Syariah Courts*, Nordic Institute of Asian Studies Monograph Series, no. 75 (Surrey, U.K.: Curzon Press, 1997).
- Syed Tahir Mahmood, *Statutes of Personal Law in Islamic Countries: History, Texts, and Analysis,* 2nd rev. ed. (New Delhi: India and Islam Research Council, 1995).
- Abdul Matin, *Bangladesh: The Muslim Personal Laws* (Dhaka: Palok Publishers, 1989).
- David S. Pearl, *Islamic Family Law and Its Reception by the Courts in England* (Cambridge, MA: Islamic Legal Studies Program, 2000).

For several country-specific studies of the Middle East, see,

deal of such research is sponsored by Women Living Under Muslim Laws, an international solidarity association formed in France in 1985. This association monitors laws affecting women in Muslim communities, publicizes injustices, and links activists and academics in an ambitious Muslim personal law reform project. One spin-off of the latter in 1988 was an exchange program for Muslim women "to enable them to experience the great variety of social practices that are labeled "Islamic."[76] A collection published under the association's aegis, with Homa Hoodfar as editor, includes articles on women and personal status laws, especially marriage and divorce laws, in the Islamic Republic of Iran, Egypt, Turkey, and Saudi Arabia, among others.[77] Another ambitious project, the Law and Religion Program of Emory University's Law School, proposes systematically to cover the substance of the laws across multiple countries and regions. The program is currently implementing a global study of Islamic Family Law (IFL). The program maintains a Web site that provides region-by-region and country-by country "mapping" of the embodiments of Islamic Family Law.[78] The objective of the project is to document the precise scope and nature of Islamic Family Law in a sample cross-section of Muslim countries and communities around the world. This "mapping process" will involve an initial global survey eventually coupled with in-depth examination of about 10 locales.

A research enterprise such as that of Emory University's Law School, with its online, readily modifiable materials, is particularly suited to the continually evolving character of personal status laws in Muslim communities. Personal status law has been and remains in flux and under pressure in many places for a host of reasons, one of which is the dual character of most Muslim legal systems. The parallel existence of two legal systems has proven to be a source of contradiction and continual contention. Provisions of gender equality appear in some nations' constitutions and in many nations' civil laws on such matters as employment and education, but such provisions clash with the thrust of personal status codes based on

---

- Mounira Charrad, "Cultural Diversity Within Islam: Veils and Laws in Tunisia," in Herbert L. Bodman, and Nayereh Tohidi, eds., *Women in Muslim Societies: Diversity Within Unity* (Boulder: Lynne Rienner, 1998).
- Shahla Haeri, *Law of Desire: Temporary Marriage in Shi'i Iran* (Syracuse, NY: Syracuse University Press, 1989).
- Aharon Layish, *Divorce in the Libyan Family: a Study Based on the Sijjls of the Shari'a Courts of Ajdabiyya and Kufra* (New York: New York University Press, 1991.

[76] Annelies Moors, 157.

[77] Homa Hoodfar, ed., *Shifting Boundaries in Marriage and Divorce in Muslim Communities* (Montpelier, France: Women Living Under Muslim Laws, 1996). Another general source covering multiple countries in the Middle East is Dawoud El-Alami Sudqi and Doreen Hinchcliffe. *Islamic Marriage and Divorce Laws of the Arab World* (London and Boston: Kluwer Law International, 1996).

[78] *Islamic Family Law.* <http://www.law.emory.edu/IFL/>

tribal/customary law. In the current case of Iraq, for instance, the proposed constitution both calls for gender equality and disallows civil legislation that contradicts the "established laws of Islam."[79] It is thus not clear whether a parliamentary statute requiring equal shares of inheritance for a girl and her brother would be struck down. Also unclear is what law would apply if a wife chose to divorce in accordance with civil law, while her husband accepted Islamic law. Civil law might allow her to initiate divorce and receive alimony, while Islamic law might not. Similar confusion stems from conflicting elements in post-Soviet Uzbekistan's Family Code, adopted in 1998. Explicitly denying the legality of religious marriages, the Code states that only marriages registered in civil status centers are legally recognized. At the same time, the Code states that local customs and traditions are applicable to family affairs.

In part because of such contradictions and ambiguities, continual efforts to reform Islamic family law have been part of the process of nation-state formation and modernization in Muslim countries.[80] The policies of modernizing developmental states have sought on the whole to reduce the scope of Sharia. Although efforts completely to rid legal systems of their duality have been vain, state policies aim to reduce, within the still dual system, the more egregiously discriminatory substance of the religious-based laws concerning particular matters, e.g., unilateral divorce by men, polygamy, and the conferral of citizenship on children by men only. Such discriminatory elements within the family laws hamper the ability of women to take advantage of egalitarian elements within the civil codes, such as guarantees of rights to work, access to education, and participation in other "public" activities, including politics. Such civil laws, touching commercial, criminal, and administrative matters, were framed in accordance with the needs of modern nation-states, including the need to utilize women's talents, while

---

[79]Edward Wong, "Iraqi Constitution May Curb Women's Rights," *New York Times*, July 20, 2005. http://www.nytimes.com/2005/07/20/international/middleeast/20women.html?hp&ex=1121832000&en=09d840d1e 4d06041&ei=5094&partner=homepages

[80] Besides the monograph on Muslim Family Law by Esposito, additional useful literature on modern reforms in Muslim Family Law includes:

- Abdullahi An-Naim, *Islamic Family Law in a Changing World: A Global Resource Book* (London: Zed Books, 2002).
- Ziba Mir-Hosseini, *Marriage on Trial: Islamic Family Law in Iran and Morocco* (London: I.B. Taurus, 2000).
- Omid Safi, ed., *Progressive Muslims on Justice, Gender, and Pluralism* (Oxford: One World, 2003).
- A. Satchedina, " Woman, Half-the-Man? Crisis of Male Epistemology in Islamic Jurisprudence", in R.S. Khare, ed., *Perspectives on Islamic Law and Society* (Lanham: Rowman & Littlefield, 1999).
- Kumaralingam Amirthalingam, "Women's Rights, International Norms, and Domestic Violence: Asian Perspectives," *Human Rights Quarterly* 27, no. 2 (May 2005): 683–710.
- Aharon Layish, "Contributions of the Modernists to the Secularization of Islamic Law," *Middle Eastern Studies* 14 (1978).

personal status law, touching so-called private matters, was long left relatively free of modernizing interventions.[81]

In pushing for women-friendly reforms of personal status law, modernizing elites have always met, and often succumbed in the face of, stiff resistance. The character of this resistance, as well as of state-driven reform programs themselves, is the subject of much scholarly discussion. One prevalent theme of this discussion is a theme of research on modernization generally, namely, that the process involves a contest for power between state elites and traditional local elites, a contest that threatens the latter by threatening to undermine the control of women by the local elite's constituency of individual males.[82] Another major theme is more specific to reform and resistance in Muslim contexts. This theme turns on the peculiar sensitivity of proposals to reform Islamic family law and how such law became charged with powerful political symbolism. As Marie-Aimée Hélie-Lucas articulates this theme, Islamic family law, with gender relations at its core, has become "the preferential symbol" of Islamic identity.[83] Annelies Moors, indebted to Ahmed, summarizes the development and persistence of this symbolic status in the following, sweeping terms:

> Because Orientalists and colonial administrators have often employed the "subordination of Muslim women" as legitimization for Western presence and interference, debates about women and gender relations have acquired a particularly strong symbolic edge, with Islamic family law as a keystone of the state's commitment to Islam. This political symbolism of Islamic family law has become more pronounced with the growth of the Islamist movements from the 1970s on, which put pressure on the states to adapt family law to fundamentalist definitions of Muslim identity.[84]

Faced with the peculiarly charged symbolism of Islamic family law, as Moors further notes, governments have had to weigh the costs of pursuing personal status law reform against the benefits. In such cost/benefit calculations, including in recent contests with Islamists, women have often been the losers:

> Governments fighting the Islamists on other fronts have been willing to give in on the issue of family law, using women as exchange money in order to pacify their fundamentalist opponents.[85]

---

[81] Esposito, 25 ff.
[82] See, for example, Hammed Shahidian, chapter 2, "Modifying Patriarchy: Rescuing Women From Allah's Men," 33-66, in *Women in Iran.*
[83] Marie-Aimée Hélie-Lucas, "The Preferential Symbol for Islamic Identity: Women in Muslim Personal Laws," 391-407, in Valentine Moghadam, ed., *Identity Politics and Women: Cultural Reassertions and Feminisms in International Perspective* (Boulder: Westview Press, 1994), 391.
[84] Moors, 150.
[85] Moors, 150.

Many scholars subscribe to such accounts of the broad dynamics at work in legal reform as they offer their more detailed and nation-specific analyses of reform. Analyses of the reform of laws detrimental to women figure as part of the large corpus of mostly historical and political economy work on the building and modernization of particular Muslim nation-states. Although state actions that affect the situation of women are far broader than reformist interventions in family law, most research on the state and women devotes significant attention to such legal interventions. Typically, the work addresses factors, uniquely combined in each state, that enabled some states more than others to overcome resistance and effect legal reforms—factors such as the dynamics of kin-based or tribal groups in relation to the state, the strength of progressive women's organizations, the attitudes of the clerical establishment, and the power of Islamist movements. Such factors have all been given their due, along with "the particular ways in which national identity [is] tied in with Islam."[86]

Four noteworthy collections feature studies on female citizens, the state, and state formation in which the substance of the laws and their reform figures significantly. The collection edited by Haddad and Esposito includes studies on three regions: the Middle East, with Egypt, Jordan, Oman, Bahrain, and Kuwait; South Asia, with Pakistan; and Southeast Asia, with the Philippines.[87] Suad Joseph's collection includes studies on gender and citizenship in MENA: Egypt, Algeria, Tunisia and Morocco, Sudan, Lebanon, the Palestinian Authority, Jordan, Iraq, Saudi Arabia, the Gulf's "quasi-states," Yemen, Turkey, Iran, and Palestinians in Israel.[88] The somewhat older but essential collection by Deniz Kandiyoti includes studies of several Middle Eastern and several South Asia states: Turkey, Iran, Egypt, Lebanon, Iraq, Pakistan, Bangladesh, and India.[89] Valentine Moghadam's collection on gender and national identity includes studies on Algeria, Iran, Bangladesh, Afghanistan, and Palestine.[90]

The cases in these collections tell a story of Muslim nations' variable degrees of success in realizing a legal reform "wish list" of modernizing elites. The fullest and most enduring realizations of this "wish list" were by Turkey and Tunisia. In the process of eliminating the duality of their legal systems, these two countries realized many of the individual items of family law reform that have been sought and sometimes partially achieved in concerted campaigns

---

[86] Moors, 151.

[87] Yvonne Yazbeck Haddad and John L. Esposito, eds., *Islam, Gender, and Social Change*.

[88] Suad Joseph, ed., *Gender and Citizenship in the Middle East* (Syracuse, NY: Syracuse University Press, 2000).

[89] Deniz Kandiyoti, ed., *Women, Islam, and the State* (Philadelphia: Temple University Press, 1991).

elsewhere. Turkey, after the establishment of the republic in 1923, and Tunisia, after gaining independence in 1956, outlawed polygamy, raised the minimum age of marriage for females and required their consent, outlawed a husband's unilateral right to divorce by giving both spouses the right to seek legal divorce, and granted the mother the guardianship of minor children in the case of the father's death.[91] Iran under the Shah realized similar reforms through the use of more indirect, and more typical, procedural devices. Iran's reformed Family Protection Act, passed in 1967 and revised in 1975, retained polygamy as a theoretical possibility, but limited it to only a second wife, and made permission to take even a second wife conditional on permission of a court, and, more challengingly, permission of the first wife. Iran gave women equal rights to petition for divorce, extended women's custody rights over children, and raised the marriage age to discourage the marriage of minors.[92] Along similar lines, the People's Republic of Yemen, in the early 1970s, enacted procedural restrictions to block polygamy and required all divorces to be arranged through the courts.[93] Syria, Iraq, and Afghanistan likewise introduced reforms that effectively altered their family codes. Outside of the Middle East, reforms were also enacted, for example, in Malaysia, which abolished out-of-court repudiations, and Pakistan, under prime ministers Ayb Khan and Zulfiquar Bhutto. Like a number of other countries that went some way in legal reform, Pakistan proved to be a case of reforms that were followed by rollback. The country saw reversals of some of its reforms during the Islamization program of the regime of Prime Minister Muhammed Zia ul-Haq (1977-1988). South Yemen presents another case of reversals; when it reunified with conservative North Yemen in the early 1990s, men no longer needed the permission of the court for either polygamy or unilateral divorce. Iran, however, stands as the prime case of the conservative rollback of reformed family laws under the pressure of Islamist movements. Khomeini's Islamist revolution undid the Family Protection Act straight away and, in addition, made veiling mandatory. Still, reform followed by rollback is hardly a universal story. Morocco presents the opposite trajectory. Often placed in the conservative company of Jordan and even Saudi Arabia, post-colonial Morocco had family laws that were extremely controlling of women, drawing heavily on conservative Qur'anic interpretations and

---

[90] Valentine M. Moghadam, ed., *Gender and National Identity: Women and Politics in Muslim Society* (London: Zed Books, 1994. [Published for the United Nations University World Institute for Development Economics Research (UNU/WIDER).]

[91] On Turkey, see Canan Arin, "Women's Legal Status in Turkey," 37–52, in Homa Hoodfar, ed. *Shifting Boundaries in Marriage and Divorce in Muslim Communities.* On Tunisia, see Charrad.

[92] See Afsaneh Najmabadi, "Hazards of Modernity and Morality: Women, State, and Ideology in Contemporary Iran," 48–77, in Kandiyoti, ed., *Women, Islam, and State.*

tribal customs. In January 2004, the Moroccan senate unanimously adopted a far more liberal family code. The code restricts polygamy, and requires that divorce be granted only in court, thus curtailing men's privilege to verbally divorce their wives. Egypt is also on the verge of an often-sought reform, a change in the citizenship law that will permit women to pass on their Egyptian nationality to their children, in contrast to the current law, which stipulates that citizenship comes only from the father.

Muslim Family Law in Contemporary and Historical Practice

The complicated processes and case histories of legal reform and backlash merit the substantial attention they receive in research on the legal situation of Muslim women, inasmuch as the substance of law is part of what defines their situation. However, the substance of law is far from the sole salient issue in women's legal position. The processes of the law's implementation have received increasing scholarly attention as well, in recognition that they too are critical. An important strand in the literature on law and Muslim women consists of studies pertinent to the law's actual implementation, studies of the judiciary and of how women make use of their legal options. The most notable features of such studies of the law in practice are the novel kinds of evidence they use and their use of such evidence to expose the actual daily problems of specific societies. Such examinations of practice are in the main anthropological and historical studies, with contributions as well from policy contexts and watchdog groups.

Some of the work that addresses legal practices takes the form of relatively systematic juxtapositions and comparisons of specific legal provisions and the judicial decisions rendered under them, along with more or less full details about who brought a given case and what it concerned. One Malaysian example of such work is Nik Noriani Nik Badli Shah's *Marriage and Divorce: Law Reform Within Islamic Framework.*[94] In this study, the author's emphasis is to illuminate the meaning of particular current laws, specifically laws concerning the role of guardians in the formation of marriage, the issue of polygamy, divorce by repudiation and by judicial decree, and financial provisions after divorce. She illuminates the laws partly by means of some Qur'anic material and historical and contemporary comparisons with laws elsewhere, and partly through the description, based on court records, of numerous cases and their

---

[93] On Yemen, see Maxine Molyneux , "The Law, the State, and Socialist Policies with Regard to Women: The Case of the People's Democratic Republic of Yemen, 1967–1990," 237–72, in Kandiyoti, ed., *Women, Islam and State.*
[94] Shah, Nik Noriani Nik Badli, *Marriage and Divorce: Law Reform Within Islamic Framework* (Kuala Lumpur: International Law Book Services, Golden Books Centre, 2000).

outcomes. Such summaries of cases show that women can achieve favorable outcomes by making the most of the options available to them under existing provisions in the family law. A woman can, for example, preempt any positive court decision on a husband's application for polygamous marriage by including stipulations in her marriage contract.[95] If she has not made such stipulations rejecting plural marriage, she may turn to the court to enforce the statutory restrictions, primarily financial, on such marriage. As in much of the work that touches on legal practice, the researcher underscores the point that the legal system currently provides a broader range of possible outcomes and more justice for women than is commonly assumed either by hostile observers of the system or by religious conservatives.

A number of researchers interested in legal practice, as distinct from the law's substance, elaborate upon the various procedural options women can exploit to circumvent the apparently unfavorable letter of the law, including one option already mentioned, stipulations in the marriage contract, as well as another option, arrangements concerning dowry. Such options allow for changes in legal rights, typically with the encouragement of the state, without actual changes in the law. A study of marriage contracts in Saudi Arabia indicates that increasing numbers of urban middle-class Saudi women use stipulations in the contract to improve their legal position.[96] In the Saudi case, the stipulations most often concern the right to study and to work, but they can include a wide range. Another study indicates that even post-revolutionary Iran not only allows, but encourages the recourse to stipulations.[97] Indeed, printed marriage contract forms contain standard stipulations, namely, that a man who wants a divorce must pay his wife, if she is judged not to blame, up to half his wealth, and that a wife be delegated the right to file for divorce under specified conditions, including polygamy, ill-treatment, and non-maintenance. Conditions concerning the payment of dowry can be similarly manipulated to strengthen a woman's position without legal changes, as a study of women in low-income Cairo communities indicates.[98]

Other work on legal practice goes beyond illustrating the range of options and outcomes for female litigants. Such work, often ethnographic studies by anthropologists, also investigates more subjective aspects of women's involvement in legal affairs, their point of view as they

---

[95] For further discussion of stipulations in marriage contracts, see Ziba Mir-Hosseini, *Marriage on Trial: A Study of Islamic Family Law: Iran and Morocco Compared* (London: I. B. Taurus, 1993).

[96] Lisa Wynn, "Marriage Contracts and Women's Rights in Saudi Arabia," 106–121, in Hoodfar, ed.

[97] Mir-Hosseini, *Marriage on Trial*.

[98] Homa Hoodfar, "Circumventing Legal Limitation: Mahr and Marriage Negotiation in Egyptian Low Income Communities," 121–42, in Homa Hoodfar, ed., *Shifting Boundaries*.

strategize to achieve favorable outcomes.[99] One such study, by anthropologist Susan F. Hirsch, analyzes disputes involving Swahili Muslims in coastal Kenya.[100] The title of the study reflects the image of gender relations most commonly associated with Islamic law, namely, that a Muslim husband need only "pronounce" divorce to resolve marital conflicts, while his embattled wife must persevere in her silent endurance of marital hardships. Hirsch, drawing upon field research and testimony in Islamic courts, focuses on the language used in disputes, particularly how men and women narrate their claims and how their speech shapes and is shaped by the gender hierarchy. Women use patterns of speech that indicate submissiveness paradoxically to strengthen their position and to undermine their husbands' claims. In demonstrating this practice, Hirsch strikes a theme that is a mainstay of anthropological studies on Muslim women, namely, that they are far from powerless under Islamic law. They have options available and actively strategize to use legal processes to transform their domestic lives. At the same time, she shows that victories come at the cost of reinforcing, through women's manner of speech in court, the dominant cultural understanding of women as subordinate to men.

A hallmark of anthropologists, close observation of what goes on in the judicial system is also an approach used by women's rights activists and watchdog groups interested in the legal situation of Muslim women. Such groups, however, follow the actual rendering of judgments with an eye to documenting and correcting deficiencies and abuses in both the substance of the law and legal practice. Often formed in response to the conservatism and retrenchment of various legal systems, such groups tend to be impatient with what they regard as the apologetic stance of ethnographers. They produce instead work whose explicit goal is to promote change. An example of such work is a major 1998 collection of papers on Pakistan based on the research and field experience of the Shirkat Gah Women's Resource Centre in Lahore. The resource center carried out the Pakistan component of the action research program, Women and Law in the Muslim World, which is part of the network of Women Living Under Muslim Laws. The collection, edited by Farida Shaheed and others, describes numerous cases, based on court records and the testimony of women, including women litigants. In the process, the study

---

[99] For a collection of articles that emphasizes women's agency in Muslim contexts, including with respect to legal restrictions, see Therese Saliba, Carolyn Allen, and Judith A. Howard, eds., *Gender, Politics, and Islam* (Chicago: University of Chicago Press, 2002). This collection brings together essays from various issues of the journal *Signs* on women in the Middle East, as well as in Pakistan and Bangladesh. Of particular interest for the legal situation of women is Elora Shehabuddin, "Contesting the Illicit: Gender and the Politics of Fatwas in Bangladesh," 161–200, which documents how *fatwas* are used to control poor rural women and how they resist.
[100] Susan F. Hirsch, *Pronouncing and Persevering: Gender and the Discourses of Disputing in an African Islamic Court* (Chicago : University of Chicago Press, 1998).

ventures into sensitive areas, such as what are euphemistically called "honor" crimes and the workings of family laws as they pertain to violence in the everyday lives of women.

Similar activist and rights-oriented work on legal practice occasionally clusters on a single case, as, for example, the controversial case of Shah Bano, an Indian Muslim woman divorced by her husband in 1978 after many years of marriage. The case attracted intensive scrutiny by both activists and scholars, because of the questions it highlights about the interaction between religiously based legal systems and civil law. In the divorcing husband's view, Shah Bano was limited, in accordance with Muslim law, to three months of post-divorce spousal support. She asserted that she was entitled to significantly more liberal post-divorce maintenance as envisioned by Indian civil law. After seven years the Supreme Court issued a ruling in her favor, whose secular thrust was subsequently diluted by Congress under pressure from organized Muslim fundamentalists. Seen as an act of appeasement, this dilution led both to renewed demands to rid the legal system of its duality through a uniform civil code and to demands, often approved, by individual Muslim women facing divorce for large one-time payments in the three-month window of spousal support. The case and its aftermath have been the subject of numerous studies that typically provide the text of court rulings, draw upon court testimony, and reproduce press coverage, as well as offer analysis.[101]

The various types of research on contemporary legal practice all owe a debt to similarly focused research of an historical nature, for it was in historical work that a number of researchers broadened the types of evidence that were exploited in understanding the legal situation of women. Historians pioneered in the examination of marriage contracts and dowry conditions,

---

[101] Studies that cover the Shah Bano case include, among many others:
- Saleem Akhtar, *Shah Bano Judgement in Islamic Perspective: A Socio-Legal Study* (New Delhi: Kitab Bhavan, 1994).
- Peter J. Awn, "Indian Islam: The Shah Bano Affair," 63–78, in John Stratton Hawley, ed., *Fundamentalism and Gender* (New York: Oxford University Press, 1994).
- J. P.Bhatnagar, *Commentary on the Muslim Women: Containing the Muslim Women (Protection of Rights on Divorce) Act, 1986, the Muslim Women (Protection of Rights on Divorce) Rules, 1986, Maintenance, Etc., Etc.* (Allahabad: Ashoka Law House, 1992).
- H. A. Gani, *Reform of Muslim Personal Law: the Shah Bano Controversy and the Muslim Women (Protection of Rights on Divorce) Act, 1986* (New Delhi: Deep & Deep Publications, 1988).
- Janak Raj Jai, ed., *Shah Bano* (New Delhi: Rajiv Publications; 1986).
- Muniza Rafiq Khan, *Socio-Legal Status of Muslim Women* (New Delhi and New York: Radian Advent Books, 1993.
- Jamal J. Nasir, *The Islamic Law of Personal Status*, 3rd ed. (New York: Kluwer Law International, 2002).
- Tanzil-ur-Rahman, *Muslim Family Laws Ordinance: Islamic and Social Survey.* (Karachi: Royal Book Company; 1997).
- M. A. Wani, *Maintenance Rights of Muslim Women: Principles, Precedents and Trends.* (New Delhi: Genuine Publications; 1987).

for example, as well as in the use of court archives. The first monograph to appear based on court records was Judith Tucker's history of women in nineteenth-century Egypt, published in 1985.[102] Using Sharia court records in Cairo and the provinces on cases concerning peasants and urban working class women, she demonstrated how court materials can be exploited to illuminate the lives of non-elite women.[103] She also used collections of *fatwas* (Islamic religio-legal opinion) to get at questions of gender relations. *Fatwas* give valuable access to daily problems of a specific society, because the opinion-giver responds to contemporary dilemmas by combining his knowledge of scripture and concrete knowledge of the local scene and time period. Other breakthrough historical work on legal matters is the monograph by Amira El-Azhary Sonbol on women in Jordan, Islam, labor, and the law, and the multi-author collection edited by her on women, family and divorce laws in Islamic history.[104] Like Tucker, Sonbol examines the decisions of local jurists through analysis of court documents. By means of such evidence in Jordan, she follows the shifting fortunes of women's entrepreneurship and ability to own and control personal property. She documents the loss of a tradition of women's entrepreneurship through the emergence of the nation-state and the legal reforms it promoted, some of which had the effect of curtailing the formerly somewhat flexible and pragmatic application of Sharia law.

Research on the legal situation of women, in its two main strands—research on the substance of the laws and on their implementation—illuminates an aspect of women's overall situation. In such research, judgments differ as to what it reveals about the well-being of women and their capacity to exercise control over their lives and affairs. The substance of the laws, with its gender-based disparities in rights, still deviates from the "wish list" of reformers, but the significance of this is unclear, inasmuch as practice and substance in any case differ. Some researchers emphasize the leeway women have in practice to redress the legal gender imbalance and to shape their lives. Others stress oppression on paper and in actuality under Muslim laws and regard family law in particular as fundamental to the inequality in the gender system. Still others, such as Sonbol, document ways in which modernization, specifically legal reforms of the

---

[102] Judith E. Tucker, *Women in Nineteenth-Century Egypt* (Cairo, Egypt: American University in Cairo Press, 1986). For the observation that Tucker was first to use this material, see Mary Ann Fay, "History: Middle East and North Africa," 341–49, in Joseph, ed., *Encyclopedia of Women and Islamic Cultures*, 345.
[103] See also Judith E. Tucker, *In the House of the Law: Gender and Islamic Law in Ottoman Syria and Palestine* (Berkeley: University of California Press, 1998).
[104] Amira El-Azhary Sonbol, *Women of Jordan: Islam, Labor and the Law*; and Amira El-Azhary Sonbol, ed., *Women, Family, and Divorce Laws* (Syracuse, NY: Syracuse University Press, 1996).

modern period, have been a mixed blessing for women, sometimes actually curtailing the leeway they once could exercise in matters of personal status.

Another interpretation of women's legal situation, however, is that, whatever it may be, women are in the grip of larger social-economic forces for change whose effects in shaping women's lives on average are sufficiently profound as to override the effects of the constraints and opportunities embodied in the legal arena. Some who argue along these lines cite as a favorite example the case of post-revolutionary Iran and the issue of marriage age.[105] Under Khomeini, Iranian law was changed to stipulate that girls may marry at age nine. While this provision might have produced some instances of early marriage, it has not prevented Iran's current average marriage age from soaring well into the 20s, as people make decisions on marriage in the light of an entire set of broad socio-economic factors and changes, regardless of what the law permits.

Demographics, Health, and Education: Ongoing "Sociological Modernization"

Many of the consequences of such large-scale societal changes register in aspects of life that are the primary concerns of demography and population and health studies. Central to the condition and well-being of Muslim women and amenable to empirically focused quantitative types of research, these aspects of life include such objectively measurable matters as fertility, health, mortality, nuptuality, and literacy and education, among others. A growing segment of the scholarly literature about Muslim women, and by far the predominate share of the quantitative work, concerns such matters. In addressing these matters, the quantitative work is deployed to paint a large-scale aggregative demographic picture of Muslim women, and in turn to tell two stories of diminishing gaps, decreasing gaps in demographic indicators between Muslim and non-Muslim women worldwide and decreasing gaps in key indicators between Muslim women and Muslim men. Apart from the simple documentation of these decreasing gaps, the quantitatively oriented research also plays a part in efforts to understand the phenomena—to explain why they are occurring—by assessing quantitatively the relationship among variables, e.g., the variables birth rates, education completion rates, age of marriage, contraceptive prevalence, and employment outside the home. Such efforts to rank variables—e.g., to find the direction of causes and effect, to identify primary determinants, and

---

[105] See, for example, Olivier Roy, *Globalized Islam: The Search for a New Ummah* (New York: Columbia University Press, 2004), 76 ff.

to assign weights to secondary determinants—are prominent in the literature, because of its direct linkage with policy-oriented contexts and development actors. Policy-makers, in considering, formulating, and assessing policy interventions, need to know not only how women currently fare in measurable dimensions of life, but also to grasp the dynamics that affect them.

While policy-makers rely upon and foster quantitative work for a grasp of such dynamics, such research is not the sole contributor to their understanding. In addition to quantitative and statistical types of work, qualitative research and ethnographically informed anthropological work makes up a significant strand of the work that addresses the matters covered by conventional demography and health fields. Some of these qualitative research studies retain the narrow focus of policy interests, seeking, for example, to assess attitudes about birth control through the use of interviews. However, some of the work is much broader, using the demographic picture sketched in both quantitative and qualitative work as a starting point for full-scale exercises in the "thick description" of anthropology.

The Demographic Picture

> *If one considers the sociological evolution of Muslims, whether in countries of origin or among migrants . . . most of the data show an increasing sociological westernization. Almost everywhere fertility rates are falling to European levels (Iran, Tunisia, Algeria, and of course within the immigrant community), with the exception of Saudi Arabia and Palestine. Everywhere extended families give way to nuclear families . . . . Everywhere there is a growing generation gap.*

(Olivier Roy, *Globalized Islam*, 2004)

Drawing upon the wealth of primary statistical data compiled by international and national government agencies, researchers are able to draw a general demographic picture of Muslim women that permits both longitudinal comparisons and comparisons with non-Muslim women. Studies that provide a comprehensive picture for Arab Muslim nations based on numerous data sources include the book-length 2004 UNIFEM report, *Progress of Arab Women*, and Philippe Fargues's 2003 article on women in Arab countries and challenges to the patriarchal system.[106] Another broad picture based on similar indicators, in a study sponsored by the East-West Center's Program on Population in 1998, examines demographic issues in East Asian

---

[106] Philippe Fargues, "Women in Arab Countries: Challenging the Patriarchal System?," *Population et Sociétés*, 387, February 2003. To further supplement the UNIFEM report and the Fargues article, "Demography," see N. Rudi, *Selected Demographic Indicators of Arab Countries and Turkey* (Washington, DC: Population Reference Bureau, 2001). <http://www.prb.org>

countries, including Indonesia, the world's largest Muslim country.[107] A slightly earlier, heavily statistical work specifically on Islamic Southeast Asia is Gavin W. Jones's monograph on marriage and divorce in Southeast Asia.[108] Although highlighting changes in patterns of family formation and family dissolution through divorce from the 1950s through the 1980s, Jones' comprehensive work also examines changes in childbearing patterns, female education levels, and female participation in paid work.

The most striking findings in the demographic picture that emerges from such studies concern issues related to reproduction, namely, fertility, female reproductive health (and related contraceptive prevalence), and the age and type of family formation. These are comparatively well-studied areas even in some otherwise understudied Muslim societies, inasmuch as reproduction-related behaviors affect population change, long a central concern of development agencies and economic planners. In the studies on Muslim societies mentioned and others, the general longitudinal story is one of accelerating reductions in the differences in reproduction-related aspects of life between Muslims and non-Muslims. In the quite recent past, demographic research revealed significant differences on average between Muslim-majority and other societies at comparable levels of national income. Muslim women exhibited relatively high fertility, as well as high maternal mortality, and female disadvantage in infant and child survival. Current research, by contrast, allows researchers frequently to speak of a "demographic transition" that is underway in many Muslim areas, a transition that belies notions of their uniqueness. The theory of "demographic transition" was originally formulated in connection with Europe's sudden shift in the late nineteenth century from high to low average fertility. The theory, which has governed population policies since the 1970s, holds that societies in general eventually abandon the strategy of high fertility when mortality drops because of health improvements and the pressures of urbanization and modernization. For demographic researchers, the evidence of Muslim countries bears out this theory, in that most have seen both fertility decline, often sharp, and improvements in child survival and overall life expectancy.

---

[107] S. B. Westley and Andrew Mason, "Women Are Key Players in the Economies of East and Southeast Asia," *Asia Pacific Population Policy* 44 (January 1998): 1–4. <http://www.ncbi.nlm.nih.gov/entrez/query.fcgi?cmd=Retrieve&db=PubMed&list_uids=12293729&dopt=Abstrac> For a collection that examines the same six countries, including Indonesia, and addresses similar issues, see Andrew Mason, ed., *Population Change and Economic Development in East Asia: Challenges Met, Opportunities Seized* (Stanford: Contemporary Issues in Asia and the Pacific, Stanford University Press, 2001). Available online at <http://www.sup.org>
[108] Gavin W. Jones, *Marriage and Divorce in Islamic South-East Asia* (Kuala Lumpur: Oxford University Press, 1994). Jones has also edited a forthcoming collection, Gavin W. Jones, and Mehtab S. Karim, eds., *Islam, the State and Population* (Karachi: Oxford University Press, 2005).

With regard to the latter, MENA, for instance, has seen across-the-board gains for both men and women, with gains for women from a life expectancy of 58 years in 1980 to 69 years in 2000.[109] As for fertility, with a slight time lag, but in the space of one generation, Muslim women have reduced their average lifetime fertility significantly and across multiple regions.[110] Speaking of Arab women, French demographer Philippe Fargues pointed to a fertility rate of 3.4 children per woman in 2000, calling it "still high compared to the world average (2.7) . . .[but] low compared to the six to eight children per woman which was the norm for the previous generation."[111] Fargues remarked further on this decline, highlighting its rapidity,

> In various parts of the Islamic world, recent demographic changes have been surprisingly fast. In countries such as Morocco in the 1980s, Algeria and Libya in the 1990s, changes in fertility have been so rapid that statistics produced by international agencies continuously lagged behind true evolutions.[112]

Elaborating upon the rapidity of the demographic transition, Fargues cites the example of Iran, the same country remarked upon in a similar context by Roy:

> It is the Islamic Republic of Iran that has experienced the fastest fertility transition ever recorded in history, with a drop from a pre-transitional 6.40 children per woman in 1986, to a below-replacement level of 2.06 in 1998.[113]

Along with addressing the general trend of declining fertility that contributes to "demographic transition," researchers have taken up the related issues of desired levels of fertility and of family planning by means of contraception and abortion. Part of understanding the demographic transition, research on these well-documented issues deploys both quantitative and qualitative approaches. Straightforward quantitative research reveals widespread growth in the rates of the adoption of modern contraceptive methods. The previously mentioned East-West Center study on East Asia, for example, finds contraception adoption rates in Indonesia of 52 percent, lower than the 74 percent rate of high-scoring Taiwan, but still a strong indication of contraception's acceptability. With respect to Arab countries, contraception adoption, as Rudi

---

[109] World Bank, *Gender and Development in the Middle East and North Africa: Women in the Public Sphere* (Washington DC: Social and Economic Development Department, 2004b).
[110] On Southeast Asia, for example, see Gavin Jones.
[111] Fargues, "Women in Arab Countries," 1.
[112] Fargues, "Demography," 321-25, in Joseph, ed., *Encyclopedia*, 322.
[113] Fargues, "Demography," 323. Fargues cites as his source M.J. Abbasi-Shavazi, "Below Replacement-Level Fertility in Iran. Progress and Prospects." Paper presented at "International Perspectives on Low Fertility," IUSSP seminar, Tokyo, 2001.

points out, is highly variable, with religiously conservative Iran showing a respectable contraceptive prevalence rate of 55 percent, while conservative Yemen shows only 10 percent.[114]

With respect to establishing desired rates of fertility, researchers typically use qualitative methods, as in a John Hopkins University study of attitudes among a sample of Jordanians.[115] The aim of the study, as narrowly construed, is to ascertain the desired levels of fertility through interviews and to consider whether the stated levels prompted the adoption of contraception, a proximate influence on actual birth rates.[116] In posing such questions, the Hopkins study and similar research opens up broader questions of causality, including, inevitably, questions about what relationship, if any, Islamic religious beliefs have with reproductive decisions.

On the relationship between reproduction and Islamic beliefs, many observers begin with the assumption that "Islam" exerts an inhibitory effect on Muslim women's participation in worldwide trends of declining fertility. Giving credence to this view are not only comparatively high initial fertilities and some instances of sluggish rates of change in the nearly universal downward direction, but also a number of outright counter-examples to the broad trends.[117] Exceptional cases of high fertility that have received scholarly attention include diaspora populations, most notably, the Palestinians.[118] Other counter-examples of persisting or renewed high fertility include Islamist sub-populations in Egypt.[119] Such cases, however, in the view of many demographers, are indeed exceptions, in which a high birth rate is best explained as a strategy whose meaning is highly situation-specific. Amongst Palestinians families, according to Giacaman, high fertility is an act of political engagement and an assertion of national identity, while in Islamist Egyptian sub-groups, according to Sholkamy, it is a marker of political dissent and dissonance.[120] Such researchers are unconvinced as to the explanatory primacy of "Islam," "Islamic traditions," or even Islamic family laws, because Islam itself has proven to be adaptable

---

[114] Rudi.

[115] Michael Farsoun, Nadine Khoury, Carol Underwood, "*In Their Own Words:* A Qualitative Study of Family Planning in Jordan," *Field Report*, no. 6, October 1996. < http://www.jhuccp.org/pubs/fr/6/index.shtml>

[116] Farsoun, et al.

[117] Some of the notable laggards in the decline of birth rates include Afghanistan and Pakistan, as well as some Sahelian countries.

[118] See Rita Giacaman, *Palestinian Women: A Status Report* (Birzeit, 1997); Rita Giacaman and Penny Johnson, eds., *Inside Palestinian Households: Initial Analysis of a Community-Based Household Survey* (Birzeit: Institute of Women's Studies and Institute for Community and Public Health, Birzeit University, 2002); and Cheryl Rubenberg, *Palestinian Women: Patriarchy and Resistance in the West Bank* (Boulder: Lynn Rienner, 2001).

[119] On Egypt, see Hania Sholkamy, "Procreation in Islam: A Reading From Egypt of People and Texts," 130–61, in Peter Loizos and Patrick Heady, eds., *Conceiving Persons: Ethnographies of Procreation, Fertility, and Growth* (New Brunswick, NJ: Athlone Press, 1999).

[120] On Palestinians, see Giacaman; on Egypt, see Sholkamy, "Procreation in Islam."

on issues of family planning under wider socio-economic and other pressures.[121] Moreover,

professed ideals and actual behavior are always more or less discrepant, whatever the avowed

ideals' basis. Cases that demonstrate this adaptability of, and non-adherence to, professed

Islamic ideals include Iran and Algeria. Algeria experienced a pronounced reduction of birth

rates, reaching the line of non-replacement fertility in 2001, in the context of a rising influence of

Muslim fundamentalists, while Iran's demographic transition occurred in a society dominated by

Shia fundamentalism.[122] In post-revolutionary Iran, the originally pronatalist clerical

establishment relented on its birth control ban in response both to the resistance of women, often

backed by husbands, and to concerns about exploding population and the underemployment of

youth. The clerics found sufficient leeway in the religion to change their stance and actively

condone family planning, as elsewhere, Muslim theologians have reached consensus that family

planning is permissible or desirable. In still other Muslim societies, notably, Tunisia, Muslims

have seen fit to legalize abortion in their civil laws. An initiative in comparative research, the

International Reproductive Rights Research and Action Group (IRRRAG), investigates further

cases, namely, Malaysia, Indonesia, and Egypt, addressing specifically both how Islam shapes

reproductive attitudes and rights and is shaped by the contingencies of everyday life.[123] In

profiles on the individual countries, the researchers conclude that Islam is far from being a

consistent barrier to change in reproductive behavior.[124]

---

[121] For readings on Islam's message on family planning, see,
- For a liberal reading, Azizah Y. Al-Hibri, "Family Planning and Islamic Jurisprudence," in *Religious and Ethical Perspectives on Population Issues* (Washington, DC: The Religious Consultation on Population, Reproductive Health, and Ethics, 1993).
- For history of the issue, Basim Musallam, "Contraception and the Rights of Women," 29–38, in *Sex and Society in Islam: Birth Control Before the Nineteenth Century* (Cambridge, UK: Cambridge University Press, 1983).
- Vardit Rispler-Chaim, *Islamic Medical Ethics in the 20th Century* (New York: Brill, 1993); and "The Right Not to Be Born: Abortion of the Disadvantaged Fetus in Contemporary Fatwas," *Muslim World* 89, no. 2 (1999).
- Abdel Rahim Omran, *Family Planning in the Legacy of Islam.* (New York: Routledge, 1992).
- T. Rogers, "The Islamic Ethics of Abortion in the Traditional Islamic Sources," *Muslim World* 89, no. 2 (1999): 122–29.

[122] Fargues, "Women in Arab Countries," 2.

[123] Hania Sholkamy, "Population and Health Studies," 412–18, in Joseph, ed., *Encyclopedia of Women*, 417.

[124] Another study on decisions about family size and related issues is Sabiha Hussain, "Do Women Really Have a Voice? Reproductive Behavior and Practices of Two Religious Communities," *Asian Journal of Women's Studies* 7, no. 4 (2001): 29–69. Hussain collects numerous case histories among Muslim and Hindu female migrants in a Delhi slum. Although she finds slightly greater vulnerability of Muslim women to high fertility, the personal histories did not bear out that this is attributable to religion. The women, in fact, operate under constraints of familial variables that are not specific to one religion, e.g., strong preference for sons and little capacity to negotiate with husbands. Some factors that distinguished the Muslim women included somewhat earlier marriage, slightly later use of contraception, and significantly lower levels of education, occupation, and land ownership.

Reaching consensus that Islam is not the most salient issue with respect to the trends in Muslim women's reproductive behavior, demographic researchers have taken up the analysis of a wider array of possible determinants, striving to see if Muslim societies are like others in the variables that prove most important. About these variables, Fargues remarked, "there is a huge amount of empirical evidence" in which,

> The spread and lengthening of school education among girls always comes first in correlation with demographic outcomes. Then variables such as age at first marriage, employment outside the household, and a few others are found.[125]

A large number of studies of Muslim populations pursue the understanding of causes in the statistical manner of conventional demography. Many such studies involve a fairly technical multivariate analysis of interview or survey findings from groups in local communities. This approach can be found in a micro-level study of women in paired Muslim and non-Muslim communities in India, Malaysia, Thailand, and the Philippines published in *Population and Development Review*.[126] The authors in this study seek to test the narrow question of whether group differentials in female power/autonomy exist that could account for the observations that the Muslim women 1) had more children, 2) were more likely to desire additional children, and, 3) if they desired no more children, were less likely to be using contraception. The study, using standard assessment tools, fails to find female power differences across the boundaries of the different faiths and thus fails to confirm any pertinence to fertility levels and decisions. Other studies that seek to illuminate causal dynamics using quantitative methods deploy such methods at the macro level of nations and regions. One such study on MENA, by economist Jennifer Olmsted, examines what she calls the "fertility puzzle.[127] To account for fertility trends, Olmsted tests the comparative statistical weights of the top variables mentioned by Fargues, among other factors, including labor force participation, income, cultural factors, and government policies. Calculating the correlation coefficients of a number of these variables, she too finds that female education levels and age of marriage are highly significant.

Both factors—education or literacy and marriage age—have themselves been fairly well-measured and studied in MENA and elsewhere, as both are of interest to policy-makers and law-

---

125 Fargues, "Demography," 321.
126 S. Philip Morgan, Sharon Stash, Herbert L. Smith and Karen Oppenheim Mason, "Muslim and Non-Muslim Differences in Female Autonomy and Fertility: Evidence from Four Asian Countries," *Population and Development Review* 28, no. 3 (2002): 515–37.
127 Jennifer Olmsted, "Reexamining the Fertility Puzzle in the Middle East and North Africa," 73–92, in Doumato and Pripstein-Posusney, eds.

makers. Early marriage, or marriage before 18—a factor in population growth because it extends a woman's reproductive span—is decreasing over large parts of the Muslim world, in accordance with a worldwide trend discussed in a UNICEF report, "Early Marriage: Child Spouses." The report finds, however, that the traditional pattern in Muslim societies of early marriage is slower to give way in rural areas and among the poverty-stricken.[128] On a national scale, the pattern's tenacity is most marked in South Asia, where in 2000 in Afghanistan and Bangladesh, 54 percent and 51 percent of girls respectively are married by age 18.[129] In Indonesia, however, the proportion of women married by age 25 to 29 dropped from 96 percent in 1960 to 89 percent in 1990 in keeping with the same downward trend seen, albeit more strongly, in five other Southeast Asian countries studied, all of which were richer.[130] In Arab countries, where marriage has been nearly universal hitherto, women are delaying marriage on average by three to seven years. In the 1950 birth cohort, 75 percent of girls married under age 20, compared to just one third in the 1970 birth cohort.[131] In six Arab countries—Jordan, Kuwait, Morocco, Syria, Qatar, and Libya—10 percent of women remain unmarried at ages 30-34.[132] As pointed out in the report *Progress of Arab Women*, this increased marriage age is independent of laws and policies and the general character of the state.[133] In Tunisia, where women may not legally marry if younger than 17 and men must be 20, the average age of marriage for females has already risen to 24 years, according to United Nations data. In Libya, it has increased from 18 to 30 years on average in less than three decades, with a startling 28 percent of women aged 30 to 34 still never married.[134]

On the factor to which Fargues ascribes primacy in determining the demographic transition, namely, education, similarly marked changes are afoot across Muslim nations and regions, with especially rapid change occurring in MENA and Southeast Asian Muslim nations. As the result of investments in girls' education, Muslim nations have significantly reduced two gaps in schooling, the gap with non-Muslim societies and the gender gap. In MENA, until the late 1970s women had among the lowest levels of education in the world. Since then, girls'

---

[128] "Early Marriage: Child Spouses," *Innocenti Digest*, no. 7, (March 2001). [Florence, Italy: United Nations Innocenti Research Centre]. <http://www.unicef-icdc.org/publications/pdf/digest7e.pdf>
[129] UNIFEM, *Progress of Arab Women.*
[130] Westley and Mason.
[131] Fargues, "Women in Arab Countries," 3.
[132] Hoda Rashad and Magued Osman, "Nuptiality in Arab Countries: Changes and Implication," in Nicholas Hopkins, ed. *The New Arab Family*, Cairo Papers in Social Sciences, Vol. 24, nos. 1–2 (Cairo: The American University in Cairo Press, 2003), 20–50.
[133] UNIFEM, *Progress of Arab Women.*

access to education and female literacy have improved significantly. In the Arab world, the level of girls' access to basic schooling has risen to more than 85 percent in the majority of countries and to 70 percent in three quarters, with only three Arab countries (Djibouti, Sudan, and Yemen) facing more than half of girls deprived of primary education.[135] Arab countries with high general levels of schooling have almost eliminated gender gaps in urban settings, although such gaps remain wide in rural areas. At higher levels of education, female enrollments sometimes even exceed those of males, as, for example, in Iran, where 54 percent of recent entrants to universities were women, and in Kuwait, where in 2003 female registrations in higher education exceeded men's by 30 percent.[136] Such improved levels of female schooling eventually register as improved average female literacy. Because of past deprivation, illiteracy among females over age 15 remains high in the Arab world—between 16 and 75 percent—and women remain twice as likely to be illiterate as men.[137] However, female literacy rates are rising rapidly in most Arab and other MENA countries, and the gender gap in literacy is closing more quickly than in comparable countries outside the region.[138] *The Arab Human Development Report, 2004,* summarizes developments in education in the following terms:

> In most Arab countries women are still subject to numerous forms of discrimination. Perhaps education marks the sole exception to the rule, where girls comprise the majority at certain levels in some Arab countries.[139]

Similar improvements in female educational attainment are also the rule in Muslim Southeast Asian contexts, where, for example, women's secondary school enrollment has increased dramatically since 1960, and the traditional gender gap at that level has largely disappeared.[140]

---

[134] Fargues, 323, and UNIFEM, *Progress of Arab Women*, 5.

[135] UNIFEM, *Progress of Arab Women*, 45.

[136] El-Wasat, 2003, as cited in UNIFEM, *Progress of Arab Women*, 123.

[137] UNIFEM, *Progress of Arab Women*, 47.

[138] Jennifer C. Olmsted, "Is Paid Work The (Only) Answer? Neoliberalism, Arab Women's Well-Being, and the Social Contract," *Journal of Middle East Women's Studies* 1 no. 2 (Spring 2005): 112–41. Accessed through Proquest, August 2005. See also Olmsted, "Reexamining the Fertility Puzzle," 81, where exceptions to the general story of improvement in female literacy are mentioned, including Saudi Arabia and Syria. In these countries, the gender gap remains disturbingly large. This gap is captured in the discrepancy for such countries between their ranking on the Human Development Index (HDI) and the Gender Development Index (GDI). In most countries of MENA, GDI statistics for the region are also not too out of line with the HDI. However, in a few countries, particularly several of the richest (Saudi Arabia and Oman) and poorest (Sudan and Yemen), the gap between the HDI and the GDI is wide.

[139] United Nations, United Nations Development Programme, Arab Fund for Economic and Social Development, and Arab Gulf Programme for United Nations Development Organization, *Arab Development Report 2004: Towards Freedom in the Arab World* (New York: UNDP, 2004). <www.undp.org/ rbas/ahdr/english.html>.

[140] Westley and Mason.

Indonesia, although poor, fares well in terms of the development indicator of female literacy.[141] In South Asia, the Muslim countries of Pakistan and Bangladesh also share in the nearly universal development of improving educational attainment for females, but at much more modest level. As can be tracked in the standard source for sex-disaggregated statistics on adult literacy in Muslim countries, the UNESCO Institute for Statistics Web site (http://unescostat.unesco.org), the female literacy rates in both countries remain low, with 35 percent literacy for females over age 15 and 54 percent for those aged 15 to 24 in Pakistan, and 31 percent and 41 for the same respective age groups in Bangladesh.

Beyond Demography's Limits

These general findings on education and literacy correlate well with demographic outcomes, predicting, for example, fertility levels quite consistently, with the exception of the anomalous case of Bangladesh.[142] Bangladesh, despite its low female literacy and high mortality, has managed, through effective family planning programs, to achieve a substantial fertility decline, with 45 percent of couples now using contraceptives.[143] The exceptional case of Bangladesh, however, does not gainsay the solidity of the statistical "education-low fertility" link. The problems with this statistical link and other correlations lie elsewhere. Statistically based efforts to account for the Muslim world's current demographic situation only go so far, because statistical correlations and rankings are mute on, for example, exactly *how* education works to promote fertility reduction. Given the limitations of quantitative or statistical approaches in illuminating the dynamics of reproductive behavior, much of the work that provides such illumination is qualitative work that proceeds from, but also goes beyond, demographic questions. Such work includes qualitative studies that take the form of full-scale ethnographies. A significant example of this kind of work is the study by Kamran Asdar Ali, a physician/anthropologist, whose book, *Planning the Family in Egypt: New Bodies, New Selves*, is part case study of Egypt's family planning program and part ethnography of several rural and urban communities.[144] Ali fleshes out the understanding of reproductive issues by getting at people's thinking and attitudes, both the attitudes and subjective experiences of the targeted

---

[141] Robert Freedman, "Asia's Recent Fertility Decline and Prospects for Future Demographic Change," *Asia-Pacific Population Research Reports*, no. 1 (January 1995): 1–28, 1.
[142] Freedman, 1.
[143] Freedman, 1.
[144] Kamran Asdar Ali, *Planning the Family in Egypt* (Austin: University of Texas Press, 2002).

recipients of the state's proffered family planning services and the thinking of the state's designers of the family planning program. In the 1980s, the Egyptian state, in collaboration with international donor agencies, embarked on an ambitious population control effort in the belief that Egypt's rapid population growth was a prime obstacle to the state's development goals.[145] Between 1980 and 1992, the program increased contraceptive use from 24 to 47 percent, and reduced fertility from more than five to 3.9 percent.[146] In Ali's view, based on fieldwork in Cairo clinics and government agencies, the state's success occurred in spite of, and was somewhat constrained by, the program's underlying presuppositions. The planners, aiming to bolster contraception acceptance, sought to "modernize" the Egyptian poor by concentrating on women and persuading them to act as individual decision makers for the good of their immediate families and in the national interest. In this approach to women, the state discounted the authority of the patriarch-husband, deeming him an anti-modern and irresponsible defender of the status quo. The state posed as an advocate of women's rights in a new kind of domestic unit, a nuclear household featuring consensual companionate marriage and devoid of pressures from other kin. The state efforts thus to "resocialize" the domestic sphere met with resistance, because they rested on what Ali's research showed to be misapprehensions about poor families. Ali found, for example, that rural men cited religious grounds for their thinking less often than Cairenes and said more often that contraception was their wife's decision. Countering elements of received wisdom of the state about factors that affect fertility decisions, Ali rounds out his study by inquiring into how his poor informants view the hostility of Islamist groups, such as the Muslim Brotherhood, toward secularist constructions of population control and family planning.

Marriage, Family, Household, and Everyday Life

The dramatic changes in Muslim societies that the large literature on demography documents are both disruptive of, and manifest disruption in, the family as previously known. Whatever their causal dynamics, changes such as the postponement of marriage, the growing proportion of never-marrieds, declining childbearing, increasing contraceptive usage, and mass

---

[145] In Egypt, as elsewhere, downward trends in fertility rates will not immediately translate into declining population growth rates, which have been high in Muslim societies. During the 1970s and 1980s, for example, Arab countries witnessed the highest population growth rates in the world. Although fertility rates have been declining, the resulting lower population growth will affect the labor force only in 20 years time. Consequently, the Arab countries' labor force growth rate is projected to be 3.5 percent annually during the period from 2000 to 2010.
[146] Kamran Asdar Ali, "Modernization and Family Planning Programs in Egypt," *Middle East Report* 205 (December 1997): 40–4.

schooling for females spell erosion of the traditional kinship-based and patriarchally extended family. As Fargues says, such changes undercut key pillars of the kinship-based family structure, including simply the prerequisite of many family members. As he says,

> That system rested on . . . younger brothers' subordination to the eldest brother in sib relationships, and girl-women subordination to males within the family or marriage unit. . . . The modern trend towards two-child families—on average a boy and a girl—quite simply lessened the scope for a hierarchy between brothers, for lack of brothers.[147]

Researchers who seek to illuminate the condition of Muslim women with respect to the sphere of the family face the challenge of describing a societal institution that currently deviates more or less radically from the model of what sociologist Deniz Kandiyoti termed "classic patriarchy."[148] Alive as an idealized concept and to varying degrees as sociological reality, the model as manifested in Muslim communities features a multi-generational household, plural mating, authoritarian exercise of power by the *paterfamilias*, young age at marriage, spouses chosen by elders, the absorption of the newly wed couple into an existing household (where the bride acts as the mother-in-law's helper), and no non-household role or identity for women. In such households, females are married shortly after puberty to maximize their fulfillment of their primary role of childbearing and rearing. Early marriage also promotes consent and compliance and allows for the further socialization of girls into their unequal role, a necessary preparation for their unequal entitlement to a share of family resources, including lack of entitlement to their own products, be they children or rugs.[149] In a patriarchal context, the male is entitled to exercise his male authority by restraining his wife's movements and preventing her from showing herself in public. This male entitlement to restrict women's behavior is in part to safeguard family honor. The honor of women—and by extension the honor of the family—depends in great measure on the good conduct of female family members. The customs of veiling, seclusion or *purdah*, and separation of the sexes are practices intended to protect women's honor. In exchange for subordinate status and unequal access to resources, the woman

---

[147] Fargues, "Women in Arab Countries?," 4.

[148] On the term "classic patriarchy," see Kandiyoti, "Islam and Patriarchy: A Comparative Perspective," in Keddie and Baron, eds., *Shifting Boundaries* (1992).

[149] Valentine M. Moghadam, "Patriarchy in Transition: Women and the Changing Family in the Middle East," *Journal of Comparative Family Studies* 35, no. 2 (Spring 2004): 137–63.

is entitled, according to the "patriarchal bargain," to maintenance and protection, in a sharp division of roles into male-breadwinner/female homemaker.[150]

This model of the patriarchal family has been and remains a simplification, of course, both because of class differences among families that have always shaped the model's realization and because of variable national and familial exposure to the forces and pressures of modernization. Class-based differences, for instance, manifest themselves in key features of the model, such as the degree of female seclusion and the prevalence of polygamy, both of which are limited by low income, even if considered desirable. In order better to capture the variability of actual families and the unevenness of changes in family form and household composition, researchers on the Muslim family have elaborated the ideal type of "patriarchal family" by breaking it down into further categories. An influential typology of this kind is that formulated by Deniz Kandiyoti, who in the 1970s delineated six socioeconomic categories of family structures and women: nomadic, traditional rural, changing rural, small town, newly urbanized squatter, and urban, middle class professional. Most of these types refer to a family in transition.[151] None represent a full realization of a neolocal nuclear egalitarian family structure. They represent, instead, a more or less modernized version of a still inegalitiarian household, akin to the classic Western bourgeois nuclear family. The version of this non-extended family type found in Muslim societies has been called by some researchers "neopatriarchal" to capture the type's still pervasive gender inequities and female disadvantage. [152]

The Neopatriarchal Family and the Role of the State

In addressing the key influences and variable rates by which the "neopatriarchal" family is produced in Muslim societies, much of the research on families and women focuses on the role of the state. The shape and persistence of patriarchal family structure depends in part on state

---

[150] On the term "patriarchal bargain," see Kandiyoti, "Bargaining With Patriarchy," *Gender and Society* 2, no. 3 (September 1988): 274–90.

[151] For another discussion of definitions of Muslim families, specifically Arab Families, see William C. Young and Seteney Shami, "Anthropological Approaches to the Arab Family: An Introduction," *Journal of Comparative Family Studies* 28 no. 2 (Summer 1997): 1–13. Focusing on anthropological approaches, the authors emphasize the usefulness of a holistic understanding of the social unit identified as "the family." They ask to what degree the family exhibits a specificity peculiar to the Arab region.

[152] The first use of the term "neopatriarchy" with respect to Muslim families appears to have been in Hisham Sharabi, *Neopatriarchy: A Theory of Distorted Change in Arab Society* (New York: Oxford University Press, 1988). In Sharabi's usage, the concept of "neopatriarchy" refers both to macrostructures (state, society, and economy) and microstructures (family). He applies the term specifically to the familial and societal type that resulted from the collision of tradition of modernity in the context of oil-based dependent capitalism, a form of capitalism marked by limited industrialization.

actions, given that the family is nowhere free of state regulation. According to a prominent theme of scholarship on state formation in general, and on state-building in Muslim nations in particular, the growth of state power involves the appropriation of powers and functions that hitherto fell to families. The fate of the family in this process depends, as much research details, on the respective strengths and cohesion of kin-based local communal groups and centralizing forces of the state, strengths that are in turn determined by a host of variable socioeconomic and other circumstances. An influential and much-referenced account of the interplay of state and family power in three postcolonial North African states—Tunisia, Algeria, and Morocco—during their accession to independence is Mounira Charrad's study of women's rights.[153] Because the three states are in many respects similar, including in their history of French colonial control, Charrad has a sort of "natural experiment" in which she can isolate the "variable" of state-family dynamics for scrutiny as to its impact on each state's variant of the "neopatriarchal" family. In all three cases, modernizing elites in the post-colonial governments sought, insofar as possible, to enact policies and laws that would strengthen the position of the state. However, at times the state's agenda was best served by curtailing local kin-based power vis-à-vis women and at times by appeasing or coopting local male power at the expense of women's autonomy vis-à-vis male kin.

In the case of Tunisia, where the balance of power between the national state and local communities favored the state, the state was relatively free to link its nation-building agenda and policies to promote the "progress" of women, in particular, policies to facilitate their access to roles outside the family, e.g., as economic producers and supporters of the state. In so doing, the state enacted laws and policies that impinged on the prerogatives of local and communal patriarchal interests and families. At the same time, Tunisia went only as far as its utilitarian goals demanded, leaving women without full rights, for example, in matters of inheritance or in marriage with a non-Muslim spouse. In Morocco, where less united state elites faced more concerted tribal resistance, the state sought to bolster its legitimacy through concessions that favored extended patrilineal kin groups. Prior to Morocco's belated overhaul of its family laws in 2004, the rights and entitlements guaranteed to women as citizens of Morocco were severely compromised by their definition as minors within the family. Within the "private" sphere of the family, largely outside the purview of the state, the father or male guardian, rather than the bride,

---

[153] Mounira Charrad, *States and Women's Rights: The Making of Postcolonial Tunisia, Algeria, and Morocco* (Berkeley: University of California Press, 2001).

expressed consent to marriage, polygamy remained legal, and the husband had the prerogative in divorce. In Algeria, the state and kin group balance of power oscillated for several decades, producing a perplexing mixture of conservative Islamic family law and secular codes whose thrust was emancipatory.

Charrad's comparative study of the state-kinship family dynamics in three relatively similar societies offers a suggestive conceptualization of state's exercise of power vis-à-vis kin groups and how this exercise of power sets parameters that influence family life. Other researchers on the state have also described power struggles in which the state either challenges societal forces that favor traditional familial arrangements or seeks to enhance its legitimacy by appeasing and gaining the acquiescence or blessing of those conservative forces.[154] Either way, the societal institution of the family and the lives of women are highly charged with political meaning, the outward expression of which may be the highly visible symbol of women's dress, Islamic or Western, officially mandated or otherwise.

Attitudes and Actualities: The Neopatriarchal Family

Whatever the outcome of such power struggles in terms of the state's legal arrangements and policies, it is one influence on, but far from wholly determinative of, either people's attitudes about, or the realities of, Muslim societies' "neopatriarchal" families. Growing bodies of research on both attitudes and the actualities of families reveal a complex mixture of "traditional" and "modern" features. On the question of attitudes, a number of sociological surveys (e.g., the World Values Survey) and a number of polls capture ongoing flux and a range of opinion, including beliefs in segments of the urban middle classes very like those of Western counterparts. One noteworthy study of attitudes is, for example, the 2002 article by Mansoor Moaddel and Taghi Azadarmaki on the worldviews of Islamic publics in Egypt, Iran, and Jordan.[155] In 1999 to 2000, sociologist Moaddel and his team undertook national representative surveys of 3000 Egyptians, 2532 Iranians, and 1222 Jordanians as part of a World Values Survey project. The survey questions concerned mainly religion, national identity, family, and gender relations. On the subject of marriage, most survey respondents in all three countries attached great value to the institution, but a significant percentage of Iranians (17 percent) agreed with the

---

[154] As noted above, Mernissi is among the researchers who pursue the idea of the state's appeasement of conservative forces at the expense of women. She has analyzed Saudi politics in these terms.

[155] Mansoor Moaddel and Taghi Azadarmaki, "The Worldviews of Islamic Publics: The Cases of Egypt, Iran, and Jordan," *Comparative Sociology* 1, nos. 3–4 (2002): 299–319.

statement that marriage had become an outdated institution. On the issue of wifely obedience, only 24 percent of Iranians strongly agreed with the statement that a wife must always obey her husband, compared to 47 percent of Egyptians and 42 percent of Jordanians. Asked whether women needed to have children in order to feel satisfied, 89 percent of Egyptians and Jordanians agreed, but only 47 percent of Iranians. On the question of whether a working mother could develop intimate relations with her children as well as a non-working mother, a larger percentage of Iranians (40 percent) agreed than did Jordanians (23 percent) and Egyptians (19 percent). The overwhelming majority of respondents in all three countries objected to the institution of polygamy. Majorities in all three countries agreed that men should be favored over women in jobs, but younger respondents, especially in Iran, displayed less gender bias on the question. The survey found too that Iranians, notwithstanding their regime, placed less emphasis on religion and more emphasis on nationalism than either Egyptians or Jordanians. Iranians were also less concerned about "Western cultural invasion" than the other respondents.

Such survey findings on values and beliefs concerning families and related matters augment other ongoing work on the actual functioning of families in Muslim societies. As in the work on attitudes, the theme of the research on the realities of Muslim societies' neopatriarchal families is variability and an uneven pace of change. For every macro-level indicator of change, research on more micro levels (family, community, class) shows innumerable instances of the persistence of traditional practices and for every legal embodiment or articulation of traditional family values, such micro-level research can document a widening gap between ideals and practice. Early marriage, for example, while decreasing in macro-level statistics, is widely practiced by poor families, often reluctantly, as a survival strategy. A recent study of five very poor villages in Egypt found young girls being married off to much older men from oil-rich Middle Eastern countries via brokers.[156] In Bangladesh, poverty-stricken parents are persuaded to part with daughters through promises of marriage, or by false marriages, which are used to lure the girls into prostitution abroad. Where marriage is delayed, on the other hand, as Gavin Jones documents in his work on marriage in Southeast Asia, the older ideal of tight parental control of girls until marriage breaks down and new issues arise about the handling of adolescent females.[157] Generational relations are also strained with the education of girls not only beyond

---

[156] "Early Marriage," 6.
[157] Gavin W. Jones, "The Changing Indonesian Household," in Kathryn Robinson and Sharon Bessell, eds., *Women in Indonesia: Gender, Equity, and Development* (Singapore: Institute of Southeast Asian Studies, 2002).

the level of their mothers, but also of their fathers.[158] With delayed marriage, consent to marriage and even free choice of marital partner by females are everywhere on the increase, but, at the same time, research shows that forced marriage persists, for example, in Pakistan. Men's prerogative to restrict female mobility, whether sanctioned by law or only by social customs and norms, still compromises women's ability to work. Without family support or male guardianship, females in the Arab world, for example, still face obstacles acquiring official papers, traveling, borrowing money, or even getting medical treatment. At the same time, families across regions have strong incentives to allow their female members to take advantage of opportunities for formal employment in growing service and industrial sectors.

In view of the limitations of macro-level statistics on trends to capture variability at the micro level and especially to provide insight into family coping strategies, much of the most illuminating work on families and the situation of women within them consists of in-depth ethnographically informed studies. Carried out by anthropologists in local communities, such studies concern themselves with on-the-ground complexities and how families negotiate internal tensions and contradictory external demands. The work typically explores such questions using a combination of data collection techniques, e.g., participant observation, interviews, and surveys. A book-length example of such work is Homa Hoodfar's study on marriage in working class families in Egypt.[159] Hoodfar highlights, in particular, the functioning of the household as an economic unit, providing a detailed picture of such functioning under the following headings: Marriage, Family, and Household; In Search of Cash; Men in the Labor Market; Women and Employment; Money Management and Patterns of Household Budgeting; Nonmonetary Contributions to the Household Pool; Consumption Patterns; Social Networks and Informal Associations; and Fertility and Sexual Politics. Her work confirms other research that reveals an increasingly high female contribution to working-class budgets. At the same time, she shows that this contribution to the household economy, because unacknowledged by male family heads, is a source of friction.

In addition to ethnographic monographs, numerous smaller scale ethnographic studies illuminate particular aspects of family life. The collection edited by Suad Joseph on the self in

---

[158] Fargues, "Women in Arab Countries," 4.
[159] Homa Hoodfar, *Between Marriage and the Market: Intimate Politics and Survival in Cairo* (Berkeley: University of California Press, 1997).

Arab families, for example, focuses on intimate immediate family relationships.[160] The articles in the multi-author volume each provide a close-up portrait of a specific type of intimate family relationship: mother-child, sister-sister, brother-sister, mother-son, father-son, etc. Called by the editor studies in "psychological anthropology," the articles seek to dispel the idea that there is only one "healthy" (Western) way to experience the self in relations to others. Another, more eclectic collection, edited by Donna Lee Bowen and Evelyn A. Early, also focused on the Middle East, and specifically everyday life in the region.[161] The Bowen and Early collection includes studies based on field work of issues such as marriage and the forging of new social ties, home study groups, and ritual in post-Revolutionary Iranian society.

An example of an article, based on field research, for a specialty journal in economic development studies is K. M. Yount's study of women's power and gender preference in Minya, Egypt.[162] Yount examines the influence of women's resources and ideational exposures on their family power and desired sex of their children. Data from a household survey of 2,226 married women aged 15 to 54 in Minya, Egypt confirm the expectation that residence with the husband's kin decreases women's family power and strengthens their preference for sons. With increased education, women report weaker son preference and greater influence in decisions, but still tend to prefer sons. Women's education, paid work, and urban residence are positively associated with a variable measuring girl or equal preference and family power.

Among the special topics on which anthropologists have dwelt in filling out their picture of families and women have been the practices of veiling and seclusion, both practices subject to simplistic interpretations and sometimes charged with political significance. In taking up the issue of veiling, scholars stress the complex and multiple meanings of the practice, underscoring that the meanings require decipherment in relation to particular circumstances. According to the often-cited Homa Hoodfar, as well as others in the voluminous literature on veiling, the meaning can be relatively personal—a matter of modesty, personal comportment, and piety—or betoken self-assertion within the inner circle.[163] Some Yemeni women, for example, feel they control

---

[160] Suad Joseph, ed,. *Intimate Selving in Arab Families; Gender, Self, and Identity* (Syracuse, NY: Syracuse University Press, 1999).

[161] Donna Lee Bowen and Evelyn A Early, eds., *Everyday Life in the Muslim Middle East* (Bloomington: Indiana University Press, 2002).

[162] K. M. Yount, "Women's Family Power and Gender Preference in Minya, Egypt." *Journal of Marriage and Family* 67 (May 2005): 410–28.

[163] Homa Hoodfar, "The Veil in Their Minds and on Our Heads: Veiling Practices and Muslim Women," 248–79, in Lisa Lowe and David Lloyd, eds., *The Politics of Culture in the Shadow of Capital*, (Durham, NC: Duke University Press, 1997).

men's sexual images through camouflaging their bodies, and some women maintain the practice of veiling against the disapproval of their husbands.[164] The veil can also be a gesture of social alienation, rather than a signifier of adherence to, or support for, a religious community or movement: In the context of immigrant communities in Europe, a Muslim girl, as Olivier Roy points out, may don the veil in much the same rebellious spirit that a boy wears baggy pants.[165] Further, as in the recent voluntary return to donning the veil after years of Western-style dress, the veil can be a political statement of various kinds. Finally, the veil can be, as the "Orientalist" stereotype has it, a sign of coercion at the hands of the state, of Islamist and other unofficial enforcers, or of a woman's patriarchal kin. Each of these possible meanings have seen exploration, and continue to be explored, in the literature about Muslim women, family, and politics.

The New Work on Taboo Subjects: Violence and Female Circumcision

A relatively new body of scholarship that gives insight into the functioning of Muslim families focuses on how familial gender-based inequality disadvantages females in their physical well-being (and psychological health). More specifically, this new work focuses on the sensitive issue of violence against women, a contributor to sub-optimal health.

Although violence has hitherto been understudied as a contributor, negative health consequences that are rooted in gender inequality in families have long been a focus of public health research in developing countries, including Muslim countries. Such health consequences register in statistics on mortality and morbidity.[166] It is mostly within families that the actions occur that lead to the world's estimated 60 to 100 million "missing" women and girls. Research in South Asian nations, including predominantly Muslim Pakistan and India, as well as in East Asian nations (China, Taiwan, and South Korea) and some sub-Saharan countries has shown the ratio of men to women to be "higher than would be expected from the typical sex ratio at birth

---

[164] "Women & Gender in Middle East Studies: A Roundtable Discussion," *Middle East Report 205.* <http//www.merip.org/mer/mer205/ellen.htm>

[165] Roy, 192ff.

[166] A large body of public health research now exists on gender-based differentials in health worldwide, much of it sponsored or supported by the World Health Organization and other international organizations. An example of an online posting of analysis of findings is World Health Organization, Department of Reproductive Health and Research (RHR), *Gender and Health,* Technical paper, no. 16, 1998. Reference: WHO/FRH/WHD/98.16. For a guide to the voluminous research by the WHO and other organizations on women and health in developing counties, see <http://www.who.int/reproductive-health/publications/highlights/highlights_hrp_2004.html> and

and the typical differential mortality."[167] Pakistan and Bangladesh, until recently, had the dubious distinction of being among the few nations where men on average outlived women, a demographic phenomenon not seen in the West since the Middle Ages.[168] Although excess female death in both countries shows some recent improvement, in keeping with worldwide trends of health improvements for women, both countries have smaller than average female-male mortality differentials, indicating below-average provision to women of the means for good health.

Violence against females, universally under-reported, and, until recently, under-researched, influences female morbidity and mortality and has become a new priority area for research. The purpose of the new research is twofold. The research serves to support and evaluate public health interventions and, going beyond this obvious immediate aim, also serves to illuminate the familial and societal situation of women more broadly. The types of violence studied include forms that are prevalent worldwide, such as domestic violence and rape, and forms that are geographically or culturally specific, such as honor killings, dowry deaths, acid throwing, and female genital mutilation. Although such abuses are fraught with taboos that pose barriers to their disclosure and examination, the magnitude and seriousness of violence against women as both a public-health issue with development costs and a violation of human rights has recently been recognized at the level of international organizations such as the United Nations and the World Health Organization and in national agencies and medical organizations. In 1994, the U.N.'s Commission on Human Rights appointed a special rapporteur on violence against women, and both UNICEF and the UN Development Fund for Women (UNIFEM) have programs in place to address the issue. In July 1997, for the first time, UNICEF included in its annual Progress of Nations report a specific section on violence against women. Along with the usual economic and quality of life indicators, progress is now also defined according to the degree of protection women have against discrimination and violence.[169] Violence—whether domestic or the special victimization of women by warfare and forced migration—is also now being addressed both in international human rights conventions and in national policies. Nations that are signatories to such conventions oblige themselves to remedy the anti-female bias in their

---

[167] Charlotte Watts and Cathy Zimmerman, "Violence Against Women: Global Scope and Magnitude," *The Lancet* 359, no. 9313 (April 6, 2002): 1232–39. Accessed through Proquest, September 2005.

[168] As of 2001, men still outlived women in only a few Asian (Afghanistan, Nepal, and Papua-New Guinea) and Southern Africa (Namibia and Zimbabwe) countries. Elsewhere, gender inequalities to the disadvantage of females manifest themselves as a smaller than expected female advantage in life expectancy. See Jennifer Jones, "Around the Globe, Women Outlive Men," 2001, Population Reference Bureau Web site <http://ww.prb.org>

laws on violence, which often fail to criminalize domestic violence, or sanction lenient punishments for male perpetrators if they act "with justification" or out of passion.

The official recognition of the seriousness of gender-based violence has provided the impetus, including in Muslim communities, to develop more accurate data on its prevalence, and a better grasp of its dynamics. A good deal of statistical information is now available, collected by international organizations, international human rights groups, such as Amnesty International and Human Rights Watch, and, where civil society organizations exist, national human rights groups, such as Pakistan's Human Rights Commission, and local NGOs, such as Iraqi Kurdistan's REWAN. These organizations produce regular reports—drawing on police and shelter records and government and other estimates—on the incidence of violence and on particular cases, as well as on the progress of legal reform.[170]

In addition to such human rights reports, a growing body of scholarship has developed that goes beyond the description of violence to explore its ramifications and causal dynamics.[171] A typical study that explores how the health status of women and domestic violence are related focuses on Bedouin Arab women in Israel.[172] In this relatively small-scale study, the researchers conducted face-to-face interviews with 202 Bedouin Arab women ranging in age from 22 to 75. The researchers elicited self-reports from the women about their health status and the impact on their health of two features of contemporary Bedouin Arab social mores: the social acceptance of domestic violence and the emphasis on maintaining a high rate of fertility. Of the respondents, 48 percent reported a lifetime exposure to physical violence, and 30 percent reported domestic violence as a contributor to poor mental health status and gynecological problems. Domestic violence was associated with a large number of children, and there is some indication that the level of domestic violence decreases during pregnancy.

---

[169] Gill Marcus, "On Women in South Africa," August 8, 1997. <http://gos.sbc.edu/m/marcus.html>

[170] Joining in the efforts currently underway to track systematically legal reform concerning violence, Emory University School of Law has begun to include materials on the subject on its Web site. On this site, see Lisa Hajjar, "Domestic Violence and Sharia: A Comparative Study of Muslim Societies in the Middle East, Africa and Asia." <http://www.law.emory.edu/IFL/>

[171] See, for example, Shahrzad Mojab and Nahla Abdo, eds., *Violence in the Name of Honour: Theoretical and Political Challenges* (Istanbul : Istanbul Bilgi Üniversitesi Yayinlari, 2004).

[172] Julie Cwikel, Rachel Lev Wiesel, and Alean Al-Krenawi, "The Physical and Psychosocial Health of Bedouin Arab Women of the Negev Area of Israel: The Impact of High Fertility and Pervasive Domestic Violence," *Violence Against Women* 9, no. 2 (February 2003): 240–58.

Another larger study focuses not on the health impact of domestic violence but on the socioeconomic risk factors for it, specifically in rural Bangladesh.[173] The research, conducted in 2001 to 2002, involved surveys, in-depth interviews, and small group discussions with 1,200 married women from six Bangladeshi villages. The researchers sought to establish the types and severity of domestic violence and to explore the ways in which the women's socio-economic circumstances influenced their vulnerability to violence in marriage. The research assessed the women's odds of experiencing domestic violence in the past year by logistic regression analysis. The research found that 67 percent of the women surveyed had experienced domestic violence at some time and that 35 percent had encountered it in the past year. As revealed by the qualitative findings, the women respondents expected women with more education and income to be less vulnerable to domestic violence. They also believed that having a dowry or a registered marriage would strengthen the position of a woman in her marriage. The researchers found, however, that, of these potential factors, only education was associated with significantly reduced odds of violence. Contrary to expectation, the odds of experiencing violence increased for women who had a dowry agreement or had personal earnings that contributed more than nominally to the marital household. Perhaps appreciating the empowering role of education, the women strongly supported educating their daughters. At the same time, they acknowledged the persistence of pressures to marry them early, including the benefit of incurring diminished dowry costs.

Similar research on domestic violence has been carried out in many regions and communities. A body of work has developed, for example, that focuses on the causes and impact of violence against women in Muslim immigrant communities in various locations, including the United States.[174] A Turkish study compares violent and non-violent families.[175] Work in Pakistan is ongoing, because of the presence of a number of local human rights groups,

---

[173] Lisa M. Bates, Sidney Ruth Schuler, Farzana Islam, Md Khairul Islam, "Socioeconomic Factors and Processes Associated with Domestic Violence in Rural Bangladesh," *International Family Planning Perspectives* 30, no. 4 (December 2004): 190–99.

[174] On family violence against women in Muslim communities in the United States, see Dena Saadat Hassouneh-Phillips, "Marriage Is Half of Faith and the Rest Is Fear of Allah:" *Violence Against Women* 7 no. 8 (2001): 927–46. Using qualitative methods, including interviews, Hassouneh-Phillips examines culturally specific marriage practices of American Muslim women and the ways that these practices intertwine with the women's abuse experiences. She confirms the expectation that Muslim women are less likely than others to seek help outside the family, for fear of disrupting communal bonds.

[175] S. Yuksel, "A Comparison of Violent and Non-Violent Families," in Sirin Tekeli, ed., *Women in Modern Turkish Society: A Reader* (London: Zed Books, 1995).

which sponsor reports, among them, a study by Yasmeen Hassan.[176] Hassan characterizes the problem of domestic violence in Pakistan as one of "mammoth proportions," affecting as many as 80 percent of women.[177]

In addition and related to the sensitive subject of gender-based familial violence is a particularly perplexing manifestation of violence, that of "honor killing." Discussed in Yasmeen Hassan's report, violence and killing associated with the honor code is more geographically specific than ordinary domestic violence. Honor killings are seen most often in Mediterranean and South Asian populations, both Muslim and non-Muslim, just as two other forms of family violence, dowry murders and acid throwing, are largely confined to South Asian populations, Muslim and non-Muslim. Honor killings occur in cultures in which family honor has great importance, women are the embodiment of the family's honor, and men claim the right to defend their own honor by maintaining the honor of their female relatives. Since the icon of family honor is a woman's purity, men have the obligation to safeguard it by various means, including virginity tests. The literature that has developed on the topic of family honor includes studies not only on the incidence and incidents of honor killing, but also on related phenomena, including the phenomenon of virginity tests and medically "restored" virginity. Representative research on the latter topics focus on Turkey, where virginity tests have state sanction and can be ordered by the state, include studies by Ayse Parla and Dilek Cindoglu.[178] In both discussions, the authors attribute the phenomena of virginity surgery and virginity tests to the contradiction between the state and familial investment in female purity and the simultaneous state and family investment in the modernity of women. Other literature related to honor and honor crimes details the kinds of sanctions to which perpetrators are typically subject. As numerous scholarly and journalistic accounts show, the cultural norms that foster honor killings are often supported by national penal codes, which stipulate light sentences for perpetrators, or by judicial practices, which impose negligible punishments. Although states have obligated themselves to remedy this state-

---

[176] Yasmeen Hassan, *The Haven Becomes Hell: A Study of Domestic Violence in Pakistan* (Lahore: Shirkat Gah, 1995). See also Shahla Haeri, "Women's Body, Nation's Honor: Rape in Pakistan," 55–69, in Asma Afsaruddin, ed., *Hermeneutics and Honor: Negotiating Female "Public" Space in Islamic/ate Societies* (Cambridge, MA: Center for Middle Eastern Studies, Harvard University Press, 1999).

[177] Hassan, 3.

[178] On state-mandated virginity tests, see

- Ayse Parla, "The 'Honor' of the State: Virginity Examinations in Turkey," *Feminist Studies* 27, no. 1 (Spring 2001): 65–90.
- Dilek Cindoglu, "Virginity Tests and Artificial Virginity in Modern Turkish Medicine," *Women's Studies International Forum* 20, no. 2 (March 1997): 253–60.

sanctioned double-standard, their progress in doing so is often slow. Governments rationalize

this slow pace by appealing to the dangers to stability of outraging conservative societal forces.

Another highly sensitive issue that has become the focus of much research is the practice,

primarily seen in Egypt and the Sudan but not exclusively Muslim, of female genital cutting.

Variously called female genital mutilation, female genital surgery, and female circumcision, the

practice is widely seen by human rights activists as a form of gender-based violence. The issue

emerged as an international concern thanks in part to its treatment by Nawal El Sadaawi in 1980,

and became a hot topic in Western media in the mid-1990s.[179] The practice in its various forms,

ranging from minor cutting of the clitoris to the drastic procedure of infibulation (about 15

percent of cases), became the focus of eradication efforts, with international health and aid

organizations placing political and economic pressure on African governments to legislate

against it.[180] In 1997, the World Health Organization stated the grounds for such eradication

efforts in the following terms:

> Female genital mutilation is universally unacceptable because it is an
> infringement on the physical and psychosexual integrity of women and girls and
> is a form of violence against them.[181]

The reasons for the less than resounding success of international eradication efforts are taken up

in a recent anthropological monograph by Ellen Gruenbaum.[182] Gruenbaum's study, based on

five years of fieldwork in Sudan, where circumcision affects perhaps 90 percent of females,

explores the meaning and role of the practice in Sudanese culture, along with the economic

incentives that tend to perpetuate it. In her view, based on observation and conversations with

women, the staying power of the practice rests partly on the ritual significance of the

---

[179] Nawal El Sadaawi, *The Hidden Face of Eve: Women in the Arab World* (London: Zed Books, 1980).

[180] Bettina Shell-Duncan and Yvla Hernlund, eds., *Female "Circumcision" in Africa: Culture, Controversy and Change* (Boulder: Lynne Reiner, 2000).

[181] World Health Organization, *Female Genital Mutilation: A Joint WHO/UNICEF/UNFPA Statement* (Geneva: WHO, 1997).

[182] Ellen Gruenbaum, *The Female Circumcision Controversy: An Anthropological Perspective* (Philadelphia, PA: University of Pennsylvania Press, 2001). In addition to Gruenbaum's study, a number of other books have recently been added to the growing corpus of work on female genital surgery. These works, which examine both the practices and their cultural meanings and Western responses, include,
  - Elizabeth Boyle, *Female Genital Cutting: Cultural Conflict in the International Community* (Baltimore: Johns Hopkins University Press, 2002).
  - Stanlie James and Claire Robertson, eds., *Genital Cutting and the Transnational Sisterhood* (Urbana: University of Illinois Press, 2002).
  - Rogaia Mustafa Abusharaf, "Revisiting Feminist Discourses on Infibulation: Responses from Sudanese Feminists," 151–66, in Shell-Duncan and Hernlund.

circumcision ceremony, and on the link between ethnic identity and the particular form of circumcision practiced by a person's group. Also, and most importantly, the practice persists, as Gruenbaum's women respondents see it, because rejecting it would dim their daughter's marital prospects and expose their daughter and themselves to increased economic risk. Such concerns override the women's desire, expressed to Gruenbaum, to reject the practice for their daughters. The women accepted the cultural belief that circumcision enhances male sexual pleasure, thereby decreasing a husband's likelihood of taking another wife, to the detriment of the economic security of the first wife. Their apparently backward-looking choice of the practice was thus a rational calculation in the face of economic vulnerability. The failure of some advocates of circumcision's eradication to appreciate this calculation undercut, in Gruenbaum's view, their eradication efforts. She sees better prospects for discouraging the practice in ongoing, low-key efforts of some Islamic leaders to spread the word that female circumcision, at least the most extreme variation, is a pre-Islamic practice, not a religious mandate.

Gruenbaum's ethnographic monograph and other studies on sensitive, hitherto understudied topics augment other research on the internal functioning of families. The new work on sensitive issues highlights the continuing vulnerability of women within families, even where demographic changes have left their mark on the family's composition. At the same time, the work on violence seconds studies of families generally in underscoring the artificiality of any separation of the "private" lives of women from the "public" spheres of the economy and politics.

Gruenbaum's ethnographic monograph and other studies on sensitive, hitherto understudied topics augment other research on the internal functioning of families. The new work on sensitive issues highlights the continuing vulnerability of women within families, even where demographic changes have left their mark on the family's composition. At the same time, the new work seconds studies of families generally in underscoring the artificiality of any separation of the "private" lives of women from the "public" spheres of the economy and politics.

- Fuambai Ahmadu, "Rites and Wrongs: An Insider/Outsider Reflects on Power and Excision," 283–312, in Shell-Duncan and Hernlund.

Women and the Productive Economy: Necessity or Empowerment?

The workings, structure, and size of the family type that some have called neopatriarchal operate within, and under the pressure of, societal macrostructures, whose operation is also a central concern within the scholarly literature on Muslim women. Many scholars who address the situation and status of women broaden the scope of research beyond the family sphere to examine the role of women in their countries' economic development and the impact of development on their lives.

In seeking to illuminate the economic situation of Muslim women, researchers face the challenge involved in researching developing economies in general, namely, that a large proportion of economic activity, especially the activities of women, consist of informal activities operating outside the recognition, regulation, and enumeration of the state. Economic researchers all acknowledge the inadequate state of statistics to capture activities in the informal sector, which encompasses paid activities in small workshops, on the street, and in sub-contracted home-based production. This inadequacy of statistics prompts researchers in mainstream neoclassical economics to devote relatively little attention to non-Western economies in general and to women in Muslim communities in particular. Such economists need large reliable data sets for the type of mathematical modeling and empirical economic analyses they prefer. They leave studies of women in non-Western communities, where most Muslim women are located, to the sub-field of development economics and to policy-oriented economic research. In these branches of economic research, the shortcomings of data are outweighed by the practical need to support the decision-making and programs of development actors in international agencies and governments. A sub-set of economic researchers within the two branches take up gender issues in Muslim countries and communities, often doing so in the conviction that the underutilization of female talent has development costs in the Muslim world.

Development economists and policy researchers are joined in the research on Muslim women by researchers in another non-mainstream sub-field, feminist economics. Feminist economics developed in the 1980s as a critique of the capacity of mainstream economics to grasp the economic situation and contributions of women. Feminist economics calls not only for improved sex-disaggregated national statistics, but also for an expanded definition of acceptable evidence in economics, as well as an expanded definition of work. For feminist economists, an adequate definition of work must encompass not only paid work in the formal economy, but also paid work in the informal economy and unpaid work in the home and community. Feminist economists advocate the use of types of evidence other than large data sets, evidence more akin to that used by other social scientists, such as evidence from fieldwork, texts, and oral histories, which are types of evidence seen by many economists as "soft," and anecdotal.

Acknowledging the problems of data availability and quality, economic researchers who focus on Muslim women often begin, nonetheless, with efforts to establish answers to the questions that are normally asked of advanced economies, where most activity, unlike that of Muslim countries, occurs in the formal sector of the economy. Such standard questions include the levels of women's labor force participation, and the levels of official support that may be instituted to facilitate such participation, such as social entitlements (e.g., maternity benefits) and support for vocational preparation. Other classic questions asked of advanced economies about women concern how they fare when they are in the labor force. Such questions concern the levels of occupational segregation and wage discrimination experienced by women and women's special susceptibility to unemployment.

Starting with questions such as these, researchers on Muslim women establish a rough picture, using whatever large-scale statistics and other data that do exist, of how women in a given country fare in economic terms compared both to male fellow citizens and to women in other countries, Muslim and non-Muslim. Researchers on Muslim women also seek to illuminate the dynamics of women's participation in the economic life of their societies, that is, to explain, for example, women's levels of paid work. The general finding of many researchers is that the levels of Muslim women's participation are best explained by the economies' need for female labor, rather than by, for example, religious ideology or cultural beliefs in male-breadwinner/female-homemaker roles. That is, for many economic researchers, economic realities and change have primacy as a shaping influence on women's economic roles and condition. In giving economic realities this priority, researchers support their stance by documenting how economies' needs have differed across Muslim nations and regions in the course of the modernization process, and as a function of variable economic development strategies. Comparing different modernizing strategies of regions and states, researchers point out, for example, that a state's reliance on labor-intensive industry for development has quite different effects on the demand for female labor than does a state's reliance on oil exports. A further body of economic research, which also grants economic forces explanatory primacy, documents how the imperatives of increasing global integration, from the 1980's on, have affected the economic situation of Muslim women.

One clear effect of globalization in Muslim countries, as elsewhere, is downward pressure on government spending and heightened international competition, both of which contribute to the increasing "informalization" or "casualization" of the labor market. With this "casualization," a higher proportion of paid work takes the form of relatively invisible, poorly remunerated and insecure work in informal production and vending. This deterioration of job quality, an economic consequence of globalization, particularly affects women, whose hold on formal sector employment is in any case more precarious than men's. This growth in informal sector employment has provided the impetus for more research on the informal sector, including in economic research on Muslim women. In this stepped-up study of informal economic activities, researchers have resorted to types of evidence beyond the conventional statistical sources, for which informal work is elusive.

In addition to researching informal sector activities, researchers on the economic dimension of Muslim women's lives also take up other questions that fall outside the usual concerns of mainstream economists. Such researchers borrow approaches that are typical of the non-economist social scientists such as anthropologists and sociologists, using them to produce numerous microlevel empirical studies, examining such topics as how female work in the cash economy affects intrahousehold power dynamics.

When Women Go to Market: Women in Paid Labor in Muslim Societies

Development economists and policy researchers who seek to draw the basic picture of women's economic conditions begin by establishing, insofar as possible, the levels of female participation in paid employment and other measurable features of their working lives. Labor force participation is one area in which women in Muslim-majority economies seem, at first glance, to live up the stereotype of Muslim women as relatively excluded from the public sphere. Women in at least several largely Muslim regions have usually low labor force participation compared to the rates in other economies with comparable economic levels. This lower participation in the economy, along with lower participation in the political sphere, is one of the few major dimensions in which women's lives in Muslim societies remain statistically distinctive compared to those of women elsewhere. Various other "gaps" between Muslim and other countries, for example, the "gaps" in demographic indicators, have been closing in recent years.

Most regions of the world now see half of the female population participating in the work force, compared to the usual male rate of about 80 percent.[183] However, according to the World Bank, in MENA, only about 27 to 28 percent of women are direct recipients of income through their participation in the labor market.[184] Other sources put levels for the Arab world at 30 to 32 percent, but in any case, the rate, although rising, is the lowest in the world.[185] The rate is lower than would be expected on the basis of the region's fertility rates, educational levels, and the age structure of the female population.

Women's participation in remunerated economic activities in South Asia also is low. Women's labor force participation rate, according to 2003 ILO statistics is about 37 percent, the second lowest level of female labor force participation in the world. Moreover, economically active South Asian women, Muslim and non-Muslim, are heavily represented in the informal sector. Sixty-one percent of economically active Pakistani women, for example, work in the informal sector.

At the same time that some Muslim women's economic lives are statistically distinctive, this distinctiveness is far from universal and is subject to fluctuations as economies change. Low female participation rates compared to expected rates are characteristic, chiefly, of the economies of MENA. Other regions, notably East Asia, including Muslim-majority Malaysia and Indonesia, have high female participation rates. In that region, women have accounted for steadily increasing proportions of total labor force growth, with economic development leading to fewer women employed in agriculture and more in both the service and industrial sectors.

Despite the atypicality of the employment experience of women in MENA, this region has been the focus of much research concerning female employment levels in Muslim societies, because of the widely held conviction among policy-makers that MENA's low levels hurt the region economically. The region suffers from its failure to capture the full returns from its substantial investment in the education and skill upgrading of its female population. Not making full use of its human capital, the region is burdened by a high ratio of working to non-working population. Such sub-optimal economic outcomes put a premium on research about the

---

[183] Zafiris Tzannatos, *Women and Labor Market Changes in the Global Economy: Growth Helps, Inequalities Hurt and Public Policy Matters* (Washington, DC: Social Protection Unit, Human Development Network, World Bank, April 1998), 4.
[184] World Bank, Gender and Development in the Middle East and North Africa (Washington, DC: World Bank, 2004). <http://www.worldbank.org/gender> See also World Bank, *Gender and Development in the Middle East and North Africa: Women in the Public Sphere* (Washington, DC: Social and Economic Development Department, 2003b).
[185] ILO, 2003 database.

phenomenon of women's paid work in the region, including its often mixed effects on women. Representative studies, among the many that arise from the policy makers' need for understanding, include a 1998 statistically based sociological monograph by Valentine M. Moghadam on women, work, and economic reform in the Middle East and North Africa.[186] Moghadam's monograph draws upon data gathered from a large variety of published sources and interviews conducted in MENA countries and compares cross-nationally the labor-force participation of MENA women in the context of global economic restructuring. Moghadam argues that the capitalist development process and, in particular, the last two decade's global trends of trade liberalization, privatization, and structural adjustment have harmed women either by marginalizing them from the productive process ("housewifization") or forcing them into it without sufficient protection and compensation (the proletarianization of women). This misuse of women, she argues, not only undermines women, but also threatens the development objectives that prompted economic restructuring. In addition to Moghadam's monograph, articles by Massoud Karshenas and Moghadam, by Nadia Hijab, and by Jennifer C. Olmsted all share her regional focus in discussions of women and work in MENA.[187] Other representative studies, also on MENA but with a specific country focus, include an article by the Institute for Women's Studies in the Arab World in the institute's journal on the female labor force in Lebanon, and articles on Saudi Arabia by Eleanor Doumato and by Kevin R. Taecker.[188] In addition to these printed works, the Social Research Center at the American University in Cairo maintains a regularly updated Web site on the economic participation, and specifically the

---

[186] Valentine M. Moghadam, *Women, Work, and Economic Reform in the Middle East and North Africa* (Boulder: Lynne Rienner, 1998).

[187] See the following titles,

- Massoud Karshenas and Valentine M. Moghadam, "Female Labor Force Participation and Economic Adjustment in the MENA Region," in Mine Cinar, ed., *The Economics of Women and Work in the Middle East and North Africa* (Amsterdam, Netherlands: JAI Press, 2001): 51–74.
- Nadia Hijab, "Women and Work in the Arab World," in Suha Sabbagh, ed., *Arab Women: Between Defiance and Restraint*. New York: Olive Branch Press, 1997.
- Jennifer C. Olmsted, "Is Paid Work The (Only) Answer? Neoliberalism, Arab Women's Well-Being, and the Social Contract," *Journal of Middle East Women's Studies* 1, no. 2 (Spring 2005): 112–41.

[188] On specific countries in MENA, see,

- Institute for Women's Studies in the Arab World, "Female Labor Force in Lebanon," *Al-Raida* 15, no. 82 (1998): 12–23.
- Eleanor Doumato, "Women and Work in Saudi Arabia: How Flexible are Islamic Margins?" *Middle East Journal* 53, no. 4 (Autumn 1999): 568–83.
- Kevin R. Taecker, "Myths and Realities About Unemployment in Saudi Arabia," *Saudi-American Forum Essay* 11 (March 30, 2003). Accessed online at www.saudi-american-forum.org/Newsletters/SAF_Essay_11.htm, on April 1, 2003.

employment, of Egyptian women.[189] The Web site has sponsorship from UNDP, ILO, and UNIFEM.

These many studies and resources on Muslim women and work document not only the relatively low participation rates in MENA, but also considerable intra-regional differences in participation, with Palestinian women having among the lowest rates, while Turkey and some North African countries boast rates that are more similar to global averages. Rates, however, are not the only concern of researchers on the region. They also study other measurable features of women's labor market involvement that are indicators of the quality of women's experience in the workforce. As discussed in the collection edited by Mine Cinar on the economics of women and work in MENA and in other research, formal sector female workers in MENA, as in many economies, have been disproportionately employed in public sector work, e.g., in civil service or in state-owned enterprises.[190] Under the state-led development strategy pursued by many MENA countries after independence, governments opened opportunities for women to fill positions in much-needed but highly sex-typed lines of work, such as nursing and teaching. As an enticement and enabling support to women to enter the workforce, some states even mandated generous benefits akin to those provided in European social democracies and socialist countries, benefits such as paid maternity leave.[191] Women, however, paid a price for such paternalistic enticements. Their receipt of special consideration reinforced cultural views of them as secondary or "B-team" workers. In the workplace, this view of women workers justified the perpetuation of women's confinement to female-dominated fields, lack of advancement to higher-level positions, discrimination in pay and other benefits, and higher risk of being laid off.[192] At home, the status of secondary earner meant no reduced responsibility for housekeeping and family care. In short, the research on MENA women's experience in the

---

[189] American University in Cairo, Social Research Center, "Economic Participation of Women in Egypt: A Resource Site on the Employment of Women in Egypt" <http://www.aucegypt.edu/src/wsite1/index.htm>
[190] Mine Cinar, ed., *The Economics of Women and Work in the Middle East and North Africa* (Amsterdam: JAI Press, 2001). [Volume 4 of Research in Middle East Economics series].
[191] UNIFEM, *Progress of Arab Women.*
[192] For discussions of occupational segregation in different locales, see the following:
- On Palestine, Jennifer Olmsted, "Men's Work/Women's Work: Employment, Wages and Occupational Segregation in Bethlehem," in Mine Cinar, ed., *The Economics of Women and Work in the Middle East and North Africa* (Amsterdam: JAI Press, 2001).
- Gulay Gülük-Senesen and Semsa Özar, "Gender-Based Occupational Segregation in the Turkish Banking Sector," in Cinar, ed.

On inequality of remuneration, see Sourushe Zandvakili, "Analysis of Sex-Based Inequality: Use of Axiomatic Approach in Measurement and Statistical Inference Via Bootstrapping," in Cinar, ed.

workforce paints a globally familiar picture in which women's unequal status in the home and discrimination and marginalization in the workplace are mutually reinforcing.

Structural Features That Explain the Labor Force Experience of Muslim Women

In seeking further to illuminate women's economic situation in MENA and other regions with significant Muslim populations, a number of researchers have taken up the question of what accounts for the variable levels of female labor force participation within Muslim regions and for the persistence of a gap between some Muslim regions and the non-Muslim world. The latter gap, in particular, has provided impetus to efforts at explanation, in view of the fact that other "gaps" between Muslim and non-Muslim women have shrunk. In turning to explanation, many researchers straightaway debunk the idea of any simple determination of women's economic experiences by the Islamic religion or any specifically Islamic gender role ideology. In rejecting this idea, they point either to the variation among Muslim-majority economies, including the variation within MENA, or to variation over time in a single country under different types of regimes.

The latter approach is central in several studies on Iran, one example of which, by Roksana Bahramitash, discusses the connection between Islamic fundamentalism and women's economic role.[193] In this study, Bahramitash speaks of, in her words, "the commonly held views about the impact of the Islamic religion on female employment" and "the commonly held belief that Islamic fundamentalism is responsible for the low female employment rate in MENA."[194] She disputes these views, arguing that, were they true, the female employment rate in postrevolutionary Iran should have declined. However, her empirical data show the reverse. Women's formal employment rates increased in the 1990s, faster than they had during the 1960s and 1970s, when a pro-Western secular regime was in power. This increase in women's employment, belated but in line with the general pattern across the developing world, suggests to her the need to look elsewhere than religion for "the most salient determining factor" of the economic experience of Iranian women.[195] In downgrading Islam as an explanatory factor, she urges that researchers examine instead "the forces of international political economy," for the

---

[193] Roksana Bahramitash, "Islamic Fundamentalism and Women's Economic Role: The Case of Iran," *International Journal of Politics, Culture, and Society* 16, no. 4 (2003): 551–68.
[194] Bahramitash, 551.
[195] Bahramitash, 552.

keys to women's labor force participation and other aspects of Muslim women's economic condition.

Other researchers—often working in the multidisciplinary field of comparative political economy—have already taken up the challenge. These researchers, including the well-known political economist, Valentine Moghadam, look to structural factors to explain women's economic experience. As a political economist, she addresses such broad-brush questions as why and how economies differ from one another. As a feminist political economist, she addresses more specifically the ways in which economies operate differently for men and women. Her approach to identifying the "causes" of Muslim women's economic experience is to seek them in the resource endowments and developmental strategies of Muslim economies, because the endowments and strategies of economies are the key to the demand for, and deployment of, female labor. Her most striking observations concern the distinctive demand dynamics that are associated with economies reliant on the oil windfall. For her and others, the oil windfall largely accounts for the lower average female employment rate in the MENA region compared to the rest of the world, as she explains in a number of recent studies.[196] Moghadam elaborates upon the role of the oil windfall on women's economic experience by comparing Middle Eastern economies that are oil-rich exporters of oil, such as the Gulf States, oil-poor suppliers of intra-regional migrant workers, such as Jordan, or relatively diversified economies, such as Tunisia. The oil-rich economies, with their higher levels of unearned income, had reduced need for earned income and thus had no large-scale need to tap their potential supply of female labor. Oil revenues permitted reliance on foreign labor for lower level jobs. Citizens who worked, able to support a large number of non-working dependents, had the option of indulging in the one-breadwinner family model. Those women who did work had the opportunity to take advantage of their relatively good education in professions and public sector jobs with benefits. In economies such as Tunisia and later Morocco, however, the development strategy was to rely neither wholly on oil exports nor labor migration, but on developing labor-intensive light manufacturing of textiles and electronics. In these sectors in "the global assembly line," women are in demand as cheap, pliant labor, and predominate in the sector's workforces,

---

[196] See,
- Valentine M. Moghadam, "Women's Economic Participation in the Middle East: What Difference Has the Neoliberal Policy Turn Made?" *Journal of Middle East Women's Studies* 1, no. 1 (2004): 110–46.
- Valentine M. Moghadam, *Modernizing Women: Gender and Social Change in the Middle East*, 2nd ed. (Boulder: Lynne Rienner, 2003).

including in MENA.[197] In short, in MENA, as elsewhere, according to Moghadam and others, women's labor force participation and experience is in large measure a function of an economy's type and predominant sectors.

In addition to broad comparative studies in political economy such as Moghadam's, researchers have contributed to a growing body of country-specific studies on determinants of female labor market participation and experience, for example, the article by Semsa Özar and Gulay Gülük-Senesen on factors that contribute to low female participation in Turkey's urban labor force, and the study by Ragui Assaad and Fatma El-Hamidi on the determinants of different intensity levels of female work in different sectors in Egypt.[198]

Apart from the research that traces women's economic situation to types of economies—e.g., oil-based or reliant on light manufacturing—researchers interested in structural explanations for how Muslim women fare economically also examine the wide-ranging economic crises and stresses that have befallen developing economies from the 1980s on. In the last quarter century, developing economies have had to cope with the expansion of global markets and trade liberalization, as well as structural adjustment programs (SAPs). SAPs are austerity programs imposed by international lending agencies, especially the International Monetary Fund (IMF), to ensure the repayment of loans. In MENA, an additional aspect of the globalization-associated crises and austerity was the cessation of the oil boom. A considerable scholarly literature has developed that analyzes the impact of these globalization-associated crises on vulnerable sectors of populations, among them women. A repeated theme of this literature, much of it from Women in Development (WID) quarters, is that the burden of responding to economic restructuring and crisis is largely borne by low-income women and women's community groups, including women in Muslim societies. A 2003 collection of studies edited by Eleanor Abdella Doumato and Marsha Pripstein Posusney addresses the effects of globalization and economic restructuring on women's economic well-being in the Arab Middle East.[199] Moghadam also contributes to the discussion of globalization's impacts in

---

[197] Carol Miller and Vivian, Jessica, *Women's Employment in the Textile Manufacturing Sectors of Bangladesh and Morocco* (Geneva: UNRISD in cooperation with UNDP, 2002).
[198] See,
- Semsa Özar and Gulay Gülük-Senesen, "Determinants of Female (Non-)Participation in the Urban Labor Force in Turkey," *METU Studies in Development* 25, no. 2 (1998): 311–28.
- Ragui Assaad and Fatma El-Hamidi, "Is All Work the Same? A Comparison of the Determinants of Female Participation and Hours of Work in Various Employment States in Egypt," in Cinar, ed.

[199] See Eleanor Abdella Doumato and Marsha Pripstein Posusney, ed., *Women and Globalization in the Arab Middle East: Gender, Economy, and Society* (Boulder: Lynne Rienner, 2003).

MENA in her article on women, work, and economic restructuring.[200] Roksana Bahramitash discusses some effects of global integration, specifically global financial integration, in Indonesia. In her article, "Globalization, Islamization, and Women's Employment in Indonesia," she presents evidence that the deteriorating situation of women in the 1990s was a consequence of the Asian Crisis, rather than a result, as some have argued, of the rise of political Islam, itself a consequence of the Asian crisis.[201] A study written by Swapna Mukhopadhyay and Ratna M. Sudarshan Kali for Canada's development agency discusses the effects of economic reforms on women in South Asia.[202]

As these and numerous other studies discuss, globalization and IMF-imposed policies disproportionately burden women in a number of related ways. Global integration and the IMF-imposed policies prompt retrenchment in overall government spending in many developing nations, including Muslim nations. This retrenchment entails cuts in government employment, reductions in food subsidies and health, education, and other social service budgets, and the sale of government assets to private interests. Privatization reinforces a general deregulation of labor markets and contributes to downward pressure on wages and greater labor market "flexibility." Taken together, lost earnings, reduced social supports, and deteriorating buying power make one-breadwinner families increasingly unviable. At the same time that female employment grows to compensate for families' losses, however, austerity measures and deregulation undermine the availability and security of formal sector employment, including public employment, increasing formal sector unemployment among women, the last hired and first laid-off. The employment options that have expanded for displaced female workers and new female labor market entrants consist disproportionately of low paid work in manufacturing for export—expanding sectors in, for example, Tunisia, Morocco, Turkey, and Bangladesh—or work in the informal economy.

Studies on Women's Participation in the Informal Economy

All of the scholarly literature on the impacts of globalization and structural adjustment programs agrees that a major consequence is the expansion of informal sector employment as a

---

[200] Moghadam, "Women, Work, and Economic Restructuring: A Regional Overview," in Cinar, ed.
[201] Roksana Bahramitash, "Globalization, Islamization, and Women's Employment in Indonesia," in Mary Ann Tétreault and Robert A. Denemark, eds., *Gods, Guns, and Globalization: Religious Radicalism and International Political Economy* (Boulder: Lynne Rienner, 2004).

proportion of total employment. In Muslim countries, as elsewhere, many of the growing

numbers of job-seeking women must settle for various kinds of casualized, irregular, and part-

time employment. This growth of the informal sector has elicited increasing scholarly interest

among researchers on women, despite the challenges the sector poses for study. The

International Labor Organization has taken up the challenge of quantifying the growth of

informal sector employment worldwide for both women and men, providing published statistical

sources.[203] Going beyond such attempts to grasp informal sector work statistically, a body of

studies is developing that illuminates the nature and conditions of women's work in the sector.

Although women are most amenable to study when they are part of the formal economy, many

researchers realize that the study of women's informal work is crucial for a true picture of their

economic conditions and contributions. For that matter, many researchers argue, no true picture

of the functioning of any economy, particularly any developing economy, is possible without

taking into account both informal sector paid work and mostly female unpaid work, work that is

uncounted and out of sight at home or in family fields.

A useful collection of articles, edited by Richard Lobban, on the informal economy and

women's participation in the Middle East covers women in numerous countries who work as

microentrepreneurs, domestic workers, home-based subcontractors, and sweatshop workers,

among other activities.[204]

Within the body of work on the informal sector generally, there is also research that

singles out a particularly challenging type of informal work to study, namely, home-based wage

work. Located in the space of the family, work carried out at home for pay shares the invisibility

of unpaid housework. A number of articles in a collection edited by Eileen Boris and Elisabeth

Prügl on homeworkers worldwide focus specifically on home work by women in Muslim

communities.[205] In that collection, Anita Weiss describes home-based work in Lahore,

---

[202] Swapna Mukhopadhyay and Ratna M. Sudarshan Kali, "Tracking Gender Equity Under Economic Reforms: Continuity and Change in South Asia," 2003 <http://www.idrc.ca/uploads/user-S/Press/IDRC2004>
[203] See, for example, International Labor Organization. *Women and Men in the Informal Economy: A Statistical Picture.* Geneva: Employment Sector, 2002. On the ILO and the informal sector, see Paul Bangasser, "The ILO and the Informal Sector: An Institutional History" (Geneva: ILO, 2000).
<http://www.ilo.org/public/english/employment/strat/publ/ep00-9.htm#Introduction>
[204] Richard Lobban, ed., *Middle Eastern Women and The Invisible Economy* (Gainesville, FL: University of Florida Press, 1998).
[205] Eileen Boris and Elisabeth Prügl, *Homeworkers in Global Perspective: Invisible No More* (New York: Routledge, 1996).

Pakistian, Zohreh Ghavamshahidi examines the lives carpet weavers in Iran, and Dewi Haryani Susilastuti analyzes home-based work as a survival strategy in rural Java.[206]

The research on the informal sector includes studies of women in particular lines of work in particular countries and localities, sometimes rural and sometimes urban. A high proportion of such studies draw upon economically informed anthropological research. Several good examples of such work focus on Turkey, which has among the highest proportions of economically active women in the MENA region, with a particularly high number of women in agriculture and carpet making, where they participate largely for informal compensation. A well-regarded study by feminist economist Günseli Berik, for example, focuses on women in farming households in rural Turkey who weave carpets that their husbands and fathers sell to intermediaries or dealers.[207] A study by economist Simel Esim on self-employed Turkish women discusses the reasons for their relatively low earnings, as compared to self-employed men.[208] Aysenur Okten, focusing on urban Turkish woman, looks at the relationship between their roles in production and political Islam.[209]

Also focusing on Turkey, an anthropological monograph by Jenny B. White examines women's labor in poor, working-class neighborhoods in Istanbul, documenting how money unites and liberates women.[210] The small family-based enterprises that White observed were often built upon kinship ties, required low capital, and had low risk. Such means, although modest, allowed women to see themselves as productive and to enhance their status, despite severe economic and cultural constraints. A similarly detailed anthropological monograph on Jordan by Shirin Shukri offers a portrait of life for women, especially economic life, in a rural village.[211] On Palestinian women and the informal economy, several studies of note include one by Simel Esim and Eileen Kuttab that discusses the levels of women's informal employment and

---

[206] In Boris and Prügl, see
  - Anita Weiss, "Within The Walls: Home-Based Work in Lahore."
  - Zohreh Ghavamshahidi, "'Bibi Khanum'."
  - Dewi Haryani Susilastuti, "Home-Based Work as a Rural Survival Strategy: A Central Javanese Perspective."
[207] Günseli Berik, "Towards and Understanding of Gender Hierarchy in Turkey: A Comparative Analysis of Carpet-Weaving Villages in Turkey," 112–27, in Sirin Tekeli, ed., *Women In Turkish Society* (London: Zed Books, 1995).
[208] Simel Esim, "Why Women Earn Less? Gender-Based Factors Affecting the Earnings of Self-Employed Women in Turkey," in Cinar, ed.
[209] Aysenur Okten, "Post-Fordist Work, Political Islam and Women in Urban Turkey," in Cinar, ed.
[210] Jenny B. White, *Money Makes Us Relatives: Women's Labor in Urban Turkey* (Austin: University of Texas Press, 1994).
[211] Shirin J.A. Shukri, *Arab Women: Unequal Partners in Development* (Aldershot, Hants, England: Avebury, 1996).

the struggles it entails.[212]   Another, by Rema Hammami, seeks to account for the absence of Palestinian women from the formal labor force in the West Bank and Gaza Strip.[213]   An edited collection on Indonesia by Kathryn Robinson and Sharon Bessell features articles on gender and equity in development, including studies of women's recent labor market experience.[214]

Microlevel Empirical Field Studies

In addition to the usually small-scale and often anthropologically informed studies on work in the informal sector, other small-scale studies, also often using ethnographic methods, address related aspects of women's economic lives. Instead of looking at employment *per se*, informal or formal, and its direct effects on women's well-being and status, these studies address such matters as the indirect effects of paid work on female empowerment. Many also address the degree to which women can access and control material resources other than earnings (food, land, income, credit, and other forms of wealth) and how such access and control affects gender relations and women's household and community power.

A monograph by anthropologist Dawn Chatty, based on extensive field research, focuses on nomadic pastoralists, economic development, and women's power in Oman.[215]   In her fieldwork among nomadic pastoralists, Chatty finds a male-female egalitarianism rarely found in agrarian and urban communities in the Middle East. The important economic roles that women play make for a complementarity of male-female roles rather than female subordination. Women take on commonly accepted male functions in the occasional absences of their male kin and display an unusual degree of independence. This independence also informed the women's relationship with tribal political organization and local government.

Pursuing themes of power similar to Chatty's, a significant body of studies in development economics examines the relationship between female assets—whether property or human capital assets—and household behavior in developing nations, often producing models of this behavior. In a study by Agnes Quisumbing and John Maluccio of Bangladesh, Ethiopia, Indonesia, and South Africa, for example, the researchers found that in Bangladesh higher

---

[212] Simel Esim and Eileen Kuttab, "Women's Informal Employment in Palestine: Securing a Livelihood Against All Odds," Working Paper 0213. (Cairo, Egypt: Economic Research Forum, 2002).
[213] Rema Hammami, "Gender Segmentation in the West Bank and Gaza Strip: Explaining the Absence of Palestinian Women from the Formal Labor Force," in Cinar, ed.
[214] Kathryn Robinson and Sharon Bessell, eds., *Women in Indonesia: Gender, Equity, and Development* (Singapore: Institute of Southeast Asian Studies, 2002).

female human capital and other assets at the time of marriage, which they equated to a woman's bargaining power, increase expenditure shares on education.[216] Another study, by Marcel Fafchamps and Quisumbing, using detailed data from rural Pakistan, investigated how human capital, learning-by-doing, gender, and family status affect the division of labor within households.[217] According to the authors, households operate as hierarchies with sexually segregated spheres of activity, in which the head of household and his spouse provide most of the labor. Daughters-in-law work systematically harder than daughters of comparable age, height, and education, larger households work more off farm, and better-educated individuals enjoy more leisure.

Another body of research in development economics examines relationships between gender and agrarian transformations. In a study of women and land tenure in Sahelian Africa, for example, Leslie Gray and Michael Kevane demonstrate that increasing commercialization, population growth, and concurrent increases in land value are diminishing women's land rights.[218] The research on gender and agrarian change also includes studies of Muslim women in the Malay-Indonesian world, examining specifically the encounter between matriliny and modernity. One Sumatra case study, for example, explores statistically the effects of a shift from communal to individualized tenure on the distribution of land and schooling between sons and daughters in matrilineal systems. The authors, Agnes Quisumbing and Keijiro Otsuka, found that while gender bias has become small to non-existent in land inheritance, daughters tend to remain disadvantaged with respect to schooling.[219] The gender gap in schooling, however, appears to be closing for the generation of younger children. Similar studies by anthropologist Maila Stivens focus on Malaysia.[220] Drawing on two decades of field work, Stivens documents the lives, work, and roles of rural Malay women of matrilineal Negeri Sembilan. According to

---

[215] Dawn Chatty, *Mobile Pastoralists: Development Planning and Social Change in Oman* (New York: Columbia University Press, 1996).

[216] Agnes R Quisumbing and John A Maluccio, "Resources at Marriage and Intrahousehold Allocation: Evidence from Bangladesh, Ethiopia, Indonesia, and South Africa," *Oxford Bulletin of Economics and Statistics* 65, no. 3 (July 2003):283ff. Accessed through Proquest.

[217] Marcel Fafchamps and Agnes R Quisumbing, "Social Roles, Human Capital, and the Intrahousehold Division of Labor: Evidence from Pakistan," *Oxford Economic Papers* 55, no. 1 (January 2003):36ff. Accessed through Proquest.

[218] Leslie Gray and Michael Kevane, "Diminished Access, Diverted Exclusion: Women and Land Tenure in Sub-Saharan Africa," *African Studies Review* 42, no. 2 (September 1999): 1–15. Accessed through Proquest.

[219] Agnes R Quisumbing and Keijiro Otsuka, "Land Inheritance and Schooling in Matrilineal Societies: Evidence from Sumatra," *World Development*. 29, no. 12 (December 2001):2093ff. Accessed through Proquest.

[220] Maila Stivens, *Matriliny and Modernity: Sexual Politics and Social Change in Rural Malaysia* (Sydney: Allen and Unwin, 1996); and Maila Stivens, "(Re)framing Women's Rights Claims in Malaysia," in Virginia Hooker and

her, the power that the ownership of land formerly conferred upon women has diminished but not altogether disappeared as women have left the land to take up urban employment in industry and services.

In addition to such research on women's assets, many studies focus on the relationship between the contributions of women's earnings from paid work to the household and intrahousehold power dynamics. Because earning power in modernizing societies tends to influence status, women's access to employment, however small the wages, can be a means of becoming less dependent on husbands and thus of exercising more assertiveness in domestic decision-making. In looking at how female employment affects intrahousehold dynamics, researchers often measure female power by women's achievement of specific outcomes in fertility control, child-rearing, and control over household labor provision and resources. Several studies on the effects of female earnings in MENA have been conducted by examining the general impact of earnings when women are major providers, and the more specific impact of such significant female earnings on marital power dynamics in working class households in Turkey.[221] E. Mine Cinar and Nejat Anbarci also focus on Turkey in a study on female employment and power dynamics in two income Turkish households.[222]

A study in rural Bangladesh by Ruhul Amin and others assesses the impact of poor women's participation in income-generating projects on their knowledge and practice of family planning.[223] The study analyzes 1992 national level household sample survey data collected from the female recipients of loans from three large rural development agencies. The study shows that the participation in income-generating projects by poor rural women has led to an increased level of contraceptive use and to a decreased level of desire for additional children.

Studies of the increased female participation in "the global assembly line" look at various effects of such manufacturing work, for example, its effects on child development in Bangladesh. Sajeda Amin and a team of researchers examine study data on Bangladeshi female garment-factory workers to explore the work's implications for the early socialization of young

Noraini Othman, eds., *Malaysia, Islam, Society, and Politics: Essays in Honour of Clive S. Kessler* (Singapore, Institute of Southeast Asian Studies, 2003): 126–46.

[221] Hale Cihan Bolak, "When Wives are Major Providers: Culture, Gender, and Family Work," *Gender and Society*, 11, no.4 (August 1997): 409–33; and Hale Cihan Bolak, "Towards a Conceptualization of Marital Power Dynamics: Women Breadwinners and Working Class Households in Turkey," 173-98, in Tekeli, ed..

[222] E. Mine Cinar and Nejat Anbarci, "Working Women and Power Within Two-Income Turkish Households," in Cinar, ed.

[223] Ruhul Amin, Jamir Chowdhury, Ashraf U. Ahmed, M. Ahmed, "Poor Women's Participation in Income-Generating Projects and Their Fertility Regulation in Rural Bangladesh: Evidence From a Recent Survey," *World Development* 22, no.4 (April 1994): 555–66. Accessed through Proquest.

women.[224] For the first time, large numbers of young Bangladeshi women have an alternative to a life in which they move directly from childhood to adulthood through early marriage and childbearing. Employment creates a period of transition that is unlike the abrupt assumption of adult roles at very young ages that marriage and childbearing mandate.

In addition to studies on the effects of women's earnings and assets, a number of studies address the means that disadvantaged people, including women, use to manage economically. One focus of such studies is the use of networks as an economic support system. A monograph by Diane Singerman, for example, focuses on community support networks, the working of the informal sector, and households in Cairo.[225] Combining the institutional focus of political science with the in-depth observation of anthropology, political scientist Singerman examines communal patterns of allocation, distribution, and decision-making among the popular classes in Cairo. Starting at the household level in one densely populated neighborhood, she maps a system of informal networks, supported by an informal economy. The informal system constitutes a layer of collective institutions within Egypt that allows excluded people, including women, to pursue their interests and meet fundamental needs, such as earning a living, saving and investing money, and coping with the bureaucracy. Through the informal system, excluded people wield influence on the larger polity and have turned exploiting the government's system of providing goods and services into an art. Other work that is pertinent to networks as an economic support system is that of Tahire Erman, who explores issues of rural to urban migration and city living for Turkish women. Erman describes the role women play both in the migration process and in establishing their lives in the city.[226]

The large and growing body of microlevel studies on aspects of Muslim women's economic lives augment the research on women's paid work, formal and informal. The body of studies is particularly pertinent to debates about whether women's increased paid work necessarily betokens improvement in women's status and well-being. Women who perform substantial amounts of paid work arguably face only a "double burden" and not an automatic improvement in their subordinate status. A precondition for improved status, many argue, is a

---

[224] Sajeda Amin, Ian Diamond, Ruchira T. Naved, Margaret Newby, "Transition to Adulthood of Female Garment-Factory Workers in Bangladesh," *Studies in Family Planning* 29, no. 2 (June 1998): 185–201.

[225] Diane Singerman, *Avenues of Participation: Family, Politics, and Networks in Urban Quarters of Cairo* (Princeton, N.J.: Princeton University Press, 1995).

[226] Tahire Erman, "The Impact of Migration on Rural Women: Four Emergent Patterns," *Gender and Society* 12, no. 2 (April, 1998) 146–64. Other work on the topic of migration addresses international labor migration, for example, that of Wardah Hafidz, who examines the problem of human trafficking of Indonesian women as a spin-off of economic migration.

renegotiation of the asymmetrical household distribution of unpaid housework and family, because the asymmetry of burdens at home contributes to inequality in the marketplace. Insofar as the microlevel studies on Muslim women's economic situation suggest that earnings, like other assets, enhance women's bargaining power, the work suggests that they, like women longer in the workforce, have an enhanced capacity to renegotiate family roles, as well as to be more assertive in the public dimensions of their lives, whether the economic dimension or the political.

Women in Muslim States and Politics

In considering women in Islamic societies in relation to the political sphere, political scientists and other scholars have taken two main approaches. One approach examines the role of the state in prescribing and shaping women's roles, activities, and spheres through state policies and laws.[227] In this approach, scholars consider, for example, whether women enjoy full rights of citizenship in their own right and have claims on social goods as individuals or have such claims only through their standing within a family. Such scholars also engage in an explanatory enterprise, examining how particular processes of state building and state operation produce strikingly different impacts on women's status and well-being. The second major approach in the literature on politics considers women as political actors, examining whether and how women participate in political processes: formal politics, including office-holding and voting, and political movements and collective action—nationalist, feminist, or Islamist—or civil society and grassroots organizations and other activities that can be considered political. The two approaches are not unrelated, of course, insofar as the marginalization of women in political processes yields state systems that operate to the disadvantage of women.

Formal Politics: Office-Holding and Electoral Politics

With respect to formal politics, which is a concern of the second approach, one finding of the literature is that the marginalization of Muslim women is relatively marked even by low worldwide standards. Two Gulf states, Saudi Arabia and Kuwait, have been the world's last holdouts in allowing only men to vote. However, that being said, researchers are forced immediately to note considerable variability across the Muslim world with respect to such things as women's participation in government as key decision makers and as members of parliaments.

This variability has been captured both in research that largely involves statistical tracking and in more in-depth local field studies by anthropologists or sociologists and in historical works.

A major source of statistical monitoring is the venerable Interparliamentary Union. Founded more than a century ago, in 1889, and now loosely associated with the United Nations system, this organization maintains various databases pertinent to women and topics of interest to conventional political science, such as the franchise and political office-holding. The Interparliamentary Union posts a table online on the dates worldwide for women's right to vote and stand for election.[228] The Union also maintains a regularly up-dated Web site, which displays current numbers of women in legislative bodies and female to male percentages by nation and by region.[229] A further resource provided by the Union is an online, keyword searchable, bibliographic database.[230]

The data provided by the Interparliamentary Union and other sources indicate that women everywhere remain, on the whole, significantly underrepresented in parliaments. In 2005, the global average for women's share of seats in parliaments (both houses combined) was only 15.8 percent. Although this percentage represents an increase over previous years, only 17 countries had reached the 30 percent benchmark recently established in international conferences, including nine non-European and less developed countries.[231] Most of these countries, including the one Muslim nation among them, Iraq, achieved the target with the help of quotas. Apart from generally falling below the 30 percent benchmark, Muslim countries show a mixed picture. Arab countries exhibit the lowest regional average of female parliamentarians in the world, with 7.7 percent. This average, however, encompasses Tunisia, ranked 33 in the world, with a percentage of 22.8, and Egypt, ranked near the bottom at 126, with a percentage of 2.9, as well as the even lower-ranked Gulf States. Non-Arab Muslim countries exhibit similar diversity. Pakistan ranks 39, with a percentage of 21, considerably higher than the 63-ranked United States, with 15 percent. Bangladesh, on the other hand, ranks 128, with a percentage of 2.0. Three Central Asian Muslim-majority states have above-average percentages, while Kyrgyzstan ranks near Bangladesh, at 124.

---

[227] For a discussion of several collections of studies on the state, gender, and the law, see above in "Legal Contexts: Women's Legal Position and Rights."
[228] Interparliamentary Union, *Women's Suffrage: A World Chronology of Women's Rights to Vote and to Stand for Election* <http://www.ipu.org/wmn-e/suffrage.htm>
[229] Interparliamentary Union, *Women in National Parliaments* <http://www.ipu.org/wmn-e/classif.htm>
[230] <http://www.ipu.org/bdf-e/BDFsearch.asp>

Such statistical findings indicate some average deficit of female legislators across Muslim countries, but the findings are so variable as to pose problems for conclusions about causes, for example, the often-assumed negative connection between "Islam" and women in positions of political authority. Similarly inconclusive are observations about the prevalence of female holders of high executive office in Muslim states. Muslim states, like others, have seen a handful of female heads of state and government. To date, these have been in non-Arab parts of the Muslim world. Female heads have included prime ministers Benazir Bhutto of Pakistan, Khaleda Zia and Hasina Wazed of Bangladesh, Tansu Ciller of Turkey, Madior Boye of Senegal, and Executive President Megawati Sukarnoputri of Indonesia. Elite women also have been appointed to high decision-making positions in Malaysia.

Apart from comparative quantitative tracking of Muslim women in high government office and of dates for receipt of the franchise, researchers interested in formal politics and Muslim women have produced a small number of more detailed studies about women in government leadership roles. The heads of state and government have been the subjects of case studies, or, at a minimum, of journalistic profiles, receiving treatment such as that of Benazhir Bhutto by Nancy Fix Anderson in a collection on women national leaders.[232] Anderson examines, in particular, Bhutto's relationship with her father as a key factor in her career, addressing more broadly the role of kinship in shaping the opportunities of Muslim female politicians. Another study on a female prime minister, Yesim Arat's article on Tansu Ciller, focuses on Ciller's use of power and whether her gender made a difference in that use.[233] Other case studies and journalistic accounts of female government heads also typically review how each female politician used power and whether gender played a role in her leadership and political career. After exploring the context and circumstances in which the leader acquired her leadership role, such studies often address, in particular, whether she used power to defy or fortify prevailing Islamic strictures on women's freedom.

Other research on women in leadership roles and, in particular, in high office includes studies on women as parliamentary representatives. Yesim Arat, in a monograph on women

---

[231] The 2005 ranking begins with Rwanda, followed by Sweden, Norway, Finland, Denmark, Netherlands, Cuba, Spain, Costa Rica, Mozambique, Belgium, Austria, Argentina, South Africa, Germany, Iraq, Guyana, Burundi, and Iceland.

[232] See, for example, the study on Bhutto by Nancy Fix Anderson, "Benazir Bhutto and Dynastic Politics: Her Father's Daughter, Her People's Sister," in Michael A. Genovese, ed., *Women as National Leaders* (Newbury Park, CA: Sage, 1993), 41–69.

[233] Yesim Arat, "A Woman Prime Minister in Turkey: Did It Matter," in *Women and Politics* 19, no. 4 (Fall 1998): 1–22.

politicians in Turkey, examines the challenges faced by Turkish female parliamentarians in the transition from the private to the public sphere.[234] The study draws upon field research in which Arat interviewed male and female members of the Turkish parliament, as well as female members of the municipality council. Abla Amawi, in her monograph on 17 female candidates in Jordan's 1997 parliamentary elections, analyzes obstacles to the women's electoral success. Drawing upon post-election debriefing sessions, she identifies as problems the disenchantment of Jordan's liberals with the electoral process and the women's difficulties in securing tribal backing.[235] A South Asian example of research on female parliamentarians is Khawar Mumtaz's study of women in Pakistan's legislature.[236] The article addresses in detail whether and how women legislators since independence have taken up women's issues, concluding only that they have done so, but without clear evidence of advancing women's interests. A discussion of women's political participation in Indonesia by Mayling Oey-Gardiner provides statistics on women in political positions at various levels, as well as background on Megawati Sukarnoputri.[237]

A further source for research on topics related to female office holding is the Organization of Women Parliamentarians from Muslim Countries, whose quarterly news magazine, *Women in Parliament*, first published in Pakistan in April 1997, prints materials pertinent to women's participation in formal politics, including profiles of female Muslim legislators and the results of field-based studies. One issue, for example, contains a survey on attitudes in Jordan about female politicians.

Such studies of women in high office are part of a broader, but also still small literature on elite Muslim women professionals. A study of such non-government professionals by Hayat

---

[234] Yesim Arat, *The Patriarchal Paradox: Women Politicians in Turkey* (Rutherford, NJ: Fairleigh Dickinson University Press, 1989).

[235] Abla Amawi, *Against All Odds: Jordanian Women, Elections, and Political Empowerment* (Amman: Al-Kutbah Institute of Human Development and Konrad Adenauer Foundation, 2001).

[236] Khawar Mumtaz, "Political Participation: Women in National Legislatures in Pakistan," 319–69, in the collection Shaheed, ed, *Shaping Women's Lives: Laws, Practices, and Strategies in Pakistan.* See also Farida Shaheed, Asma Zia, and Sohail Warraich, *Women in Politics: Participation and Representation in Pakistan* (Lahore: Shirkat Gah, 1998). Shaheed and Mumtaz are founding members and key players in the transnational feminist network Women Living Under Muslim Laws.

[237] Mayling Oey-Gardiner, "And the Winner Is . . . Indonesian Women in Public Life," in Kathryn Robinson and Sharon Bessell, eds., *Women in Indonesia: Gender, Equity, and Development.* (Singapore: Institute of Southeast Asian Studies, 2002): 100–12.

Kabasakal profiles top female managers in Turkey.[238] Another, also on Turkey, by Isik Urla-Zeytinoglu and others examines the factors that affect the careers of female managers.[239]

Women's Activism for Building the Nation, Development, and Human/Women's Rights

Because Muslim women's participation in formal politics as high officeholders and decision-makers remains low, research on Muslim women and politics has generally given higher priority to other forms of women's political participation, for example, participation in political parties and social movements—nationalist, feminist, or Islamist—and to the various ways in which women have organized themselves for group action. Such scholarly work on women in movements, organizations, and groups—often stretching the definition of the "political"—is frequently carried out by researchers other than political scientists—historians, sociologists, anthropologists, and researchers in interdisciplinary fields. Within conventional political science, as in conventional economics, women in general and Muslim women in particular remain understudied and relatively invisible.

A topic area comparatively well covered, chiefly by researchers whose home disciplines are history, sociology, and anthropology, is that of women's struggles within Muslim states for the advancement of women's rights and interests. In broad outlines, many researchers agree upon a succession of phases in such struggles. In the first phase, whose timing varied but everywhere antedated the past two decades, women were mobilized and incorporated in their nation's modern projects of decolonization, nation-state construction, and economic development. In various locales across MENA, South Asia, and Southeast Asia, as Kumari Jayawardena recounts, women, organized as groups, participated in national liberation and nation-building and simultaneously engaged with the state and its gender policies to push for greater gender equality.[240] In this first phase, as many nationally focused narratives detail, state-building elites considered nation-state construction and the improvement of women's legal and political rights to be of a piece. Greater gender parity was generally associated with national development and progress.[241]

---

[238] Hayat Kabasakal, "A Profile of Top Managers in Turkey," in Zehra Arat, *Deconstructing Images of "The Turkish Woman"* (New York: St. Martin's Press, 1998).

[239] Isik Urla-Zeytinoglu et al. "Factors Affecting Female Managers' Careers in Turkey," in Cinar, ed.

[240] Kumari Jayawardena, *Feminism and Nationalism in the Third World* (New Delhi: Kali for Women, 1986).

[241] For sources that elaborate on this integration of nation-building and women's activism with respect to MENA, see the following collections:

In the second phase of struggles for women's interests, however, women's organized efforts often became de-linked from state action. As of the 1980s, women in various Muslim countries began to form autonomous groups whose mission was to advocate and work for women's advancement.[242] These emerging groups varied greatly in their political complexion, with secular leftists on one extreme, groups affiliated with Islamic or even Islamist movements on the other, and many types of women's advocacy groups in between. The secular leftists, along with secular liberals, typically found the actions hitherto taken by states on behalf of women too limited. While state interests prompted the mobilization of women in the public sphere as either political or economic actors, state-initiated reformist actions frequently allowed women's fate in the private family sphere to remain the charge of traditional patriarchal interests. Secular advocates of women's interests also grew alarmed about the detrimental effects on women of two related phenomena increasingly evident in the 1980s, namely, globalization and the growing power of Islamism. The inadequate defense by states of women's right's in the face of these threats prompted secular women's groups to formulate independent and more avowedly "feminist" agendas. These agendas resembled and sometimes drew inspiration from the agendas of what Nayereh Tohidi called "global feminism," referring to the international women's movement that manifested itself in U.N.-sponsored venues as of 1975, such as world conferences and NGO forums.[243] At the same time that groups of secular feminists mobilized for change in various Muslim societies, religiously committed groups emerged that sought to advance women's interests within a faith-based framework. Such groups, frequently identified as "Islamic feminists" by others, usually eschewed the label "feminist" themselves, associating that term with the West and hostility to Islam.[244] Still, religiously-based groups often pressed for

---

- Lila Abu Lughod, ed., *Remaking Women: Feminism and Modernity in the Middle East* (Princeton, NJ: Princeton University Press 1998). Abu Lughod's collection includes articles on women and women's movements in many Middle Eastern countries in the 19th and 20th centuries.
- Suha Sabbagh, ed., *Arab Women: Between Defiance and Restraint* (New York: Olive Branch Press, 1997). Sabbagh's collection contains articles that concern women's rights and political participation in Algeria, Egypt, Lebanon, Jordan, Kuwait, Palestine/Israel, Saudi Arabia, Syria, and Yemen.

[242] On the distinction between non-autonomous and autonomous women's groups, see Nilüfer Çağatay and Yasemin Nuhoğlu Soysal, "Comparative Observations on Feminism and the Nation-Building Process," in Tekeli, ed., 264.

[243] On "global feminism" in the 1980s as an outgrowth of globalization and simultaneously a critical response to it, see Nayereh Tohidi, "The Global-Local Intersection of Feminism in Muslim Societies: The Cases of Iran and Azerbaijan,." *Social Research* 69, no. 3 (Fall 2002): 851–89. Accessed through Proquest.

[244] The phenomenon of "Islamic feminism" goes under a variety of labels, including, for example, "Islamic gender activism" and "Islamic gender reformism." See Nayereh Tohidi, "The Issues at Hand," pages 277–94 in Herbert L. Bodman and Nayereh Tohidi, eds., *Women in Muslim Societies: Diversity within Unity* (Boulder: Lynne Rienner, 1998), 287.

changes that overlapped with the changes sought by feminists who accepted the label and spoke in secular terms.

A third phase of women's struggle in Muslim lands has recently been singled out in the scholarly literature on Muslim women and politics. As described by Valentine Moghadam, Margot Badran, Nayereh Tohidi, and others, this phase, evident since the 1990s, is characterized by a certain rapprochement between ostensibly opposite types of activists for women's rights—the secular and the religious—as well as the growth of transnational networks of women pressing for women's advancement.[245] The third phase also features continuing proliferation of types of groups dedicated to improving women's lives. The groups include, as women's organizations have in the past, all manner of charitable and women's advocacy organizations, as described by Dawn Chatty.[246] In addition, a new and growing phenomenon, particularly in the wake of the Fourth United Nations Congress on Women in Beijing in 1995, are numerous women's NGOs, many with international linkages.[247] A number of observers regard this third phase of women's activism as a seedbed both for the modernizing reform of Islamic interpretation and practice and for contributions to the wider project of democratization in Muslim contexts.

V. CONCLUSION

Born only in the past two decades, the voluminous and rapidly expanding social science scholarship on women in Muslims societies offers an impressive corrective for the monolithic stereotypes that have long prevailed about the world's half a billion Muslim women. The scholarly literature now begins to do justice to their national, social, ethnic, and political diversity and to reflect the complexity of their lives. In so doing, the literature calls into question

---

[245] On transnational networks, see Valentine M. Moghadam, *Globalizing Women: Transnational Feminist Networks* (Baltimore: Johns Hopkins University Press, 2005). Moghadam highlights two Muslim women's networks, Women Living Under Muslim Laws (WLUML) and Sisters in Islam. Exploiting the revolution in communications, both advocate legal reform and organize resistance to Islamist threats to women's progress. WLUML includes believing and non-believing women, as well as women born into different religious communities in the Muslim world. The women associated with Sisters in Islam identify themselves as Muslim women, but favor the separation of religion and state.

[246] Dawn Chatty and A. Rabo, eds., *Organizing Women: Formal and Informal Women's Groups in the Middle East* (Oxford: Berg, 1997).

[247] For a discussion of the role of NGOs, see Valentine. M. Moghadam, "Women's NGO's in the Middle East and North Africa: Constraints, Opportunities, and Priorities," in Dawn Chatty and A. Rabo, eds., *Organizing Women: Formal and Informal Women's Groups in the Middle East* (Oxford: Berg, 1997). Significant examples of NGOs include Shirkah Gah, a women's resource center based in Lahore and headed by Farida Shaheed and Khawar Mumtaz, and the Nigerian, Lagos-based NGO, Baobaob, which coordinates WLUML's work in Africa.

simplistic assumptions about the salience of the Islamic religion in shaping Muslim women's lives. The enormous diversity of those lives belies the idea that the single factor of "Islam" could be a primary determinant of Muslim women's status and well-being. Rather, Islam itself is caught up in, and colored by, the specific histories and socioeconomic circumstances that shape the lives of Muslim women.

At the same time that the new scholarship underscores that Muslim women are enormously diverse, it underscores that they as a population also participate in worldwide trends and are not as distinctive among women as was formerly assumed. Across regions, Muslim women are on average in better health and better educated compared to previous generations, and more on a par with the men of their generation. Delaying marriage and having fewer children, Muslim women are rapidly reducing or eliminating the distinction between their marriage and childbearing patterns and those seen in non-Muslim societies of comparable levels of development. Muslim women also are closing the gap between their rates of labor force participation and those of non-Muslim women. In the realm of politics, they share with other women the experience of marginalization, and, increasingly, the determination to mobilize against it, as well as the other forms of disadvantage they experience as women.

SELECTED BIBLIOGRAPHY

Abdo, Nahla, and Ronit Lentin, eds. *Women and the Politics of Military Confrontation: Palestinian and Israeli Gendered Narratives of Dislocation.* New York: Berghahn Books, 2002.

Abdullah, Ustaz Yoonus. *Sharia in Africa.* Ijebu-Ode, Nigeria: Shebiotimo Publications, 1998.

Abou El Fadl, Khaled. *Speaking in God's Name: Islamic Law, Authority and Women.* Oxford: Oneworld Press 2001.

Abu Lughod, Lila. "Introduction: Feminist Longing and Postcolonial Conditions." In Lila Abu Lughod, ed., *Remaking Women: Feminism and Modernity in the Middle East.* Princeton: Princeton University Press, 1998.

Abu Lughod, Lila, ed. *Remaking Women: Feminism and Modernity in the Middle East.* Princeton: Princeton University Press, 1998.

Abusharaf, Rogaia Mustafa. "Revisiting Feminist Discourses on Infibulation: Responses from Sudanese Feminists." In Bettina Shell-Duncan and Yvla Hernlund, eds., *Female "Circumcision" in Africa: Culture, Controversy and Change.* Boulder: Lynne Reiner, 2000.

Ackerman, Frank, and David Kiron, Neva Goodwin, Jonathan Harris, and Kevin P. Gallagher, eds. *Human Well-Being and Economic Goals.* Washington, DC: Island Press, 1998.

Afary, Janet. "Feminism and the Challenge of Muslim Fundmentalism." In *Spoils of War: Women of Color, Cultures and Revolutions.* Rowman and Littlefield, 1997.

Afkami, Mahnaz, ed. *Faith and Freedom: Women's Human Rights in the Muslim World.* Syracuse, NY: Syracuse University Press, 1995.

Afkhami, Mahnaz, and Erika Friedl, eds. *Muslim Women and the Politics of Participation: Implementing the Beijing Platform.* Syracuse, NY: Syracuse University Press, 1997.

Afsaruddin, Asma, ed. *Hermeneutics and Honor: Negotiating Female "Public" Space in Islamic/ate Societies.* Cambridge, MA: Center for Middle Eastern Studies, Harvard University Press, 1999.

Ahmadu, Fuambai. "Rites and Wrongs: An Insider/Outsider Reflects on Power and Excision." In Bettina Shell-Duncan and Yvla Hernlund, eds., *Female "Circumcision" in Africa: Culture, Controversy and Change.* Boulder: Lynne Reiner, 2000.

Ahmed, Leila. *Women and Gender in Islam: Historical Roots of a Modern Debate.* New Haven, CN: Yale University Press, 1993.

Akhtar, Saleem. *Shah Bano Judgement in Islamic Perspective: A Socio-Legal Study.* New Delhi: Kitab Bhavan, 1994.

Al-Hibri, Azizah Y. "Family Planning and Islamic Jurisprudence." In *Religious and Ethical Perspectives on Population Issues*. Washington, DC: The Religious Consultation on Population, Reproductive Health, and Ethics, 1993.

Al-Hibri, Azizah Y. "Islamic Law and Muslim Women in America." In Marjorie Garber, and Rebecca L. Walkowitz, eds., *One Nation Under God? Religion and American Culture*. New York: Routledge, 1999.

Al-Raida, 15, nos. 80–81 (Winter/Spring 1998). [Special Issue on CEDAW and Arab countries, Journal of the Institute for Women's Studies in the Arab World, Lebanese American University, Beirut].

Ali, Kamran Asdar. "Modernization and Family Planning Programs in Egypt," *Middle East Report* 205 (December 1997): 40–4.

Ali, Kamran Asdar. *Planning the Family in Egypt: New Bodies, New Selves*. Austin: University of Texas Press, 2002.

Ali, Shaheen Sardar. *Gender and Human Rights in Islam and International Law: Equal Before Allah, Unequal Before Man?* The Hague and Boston: Kluwer Law International; 2000.

Altorki, Soraya, and C. F. El-Solh. *Arab Women in the Field: Studying Your Own Society*. Syracuse, NY: Syracuse University Press, 1988.

Amawi, Abla. *Against All Odds: Jordanian Women, Elections, and Political Empowerment*. Amman: Al-Kutbah Institute of Human Development and Konrad Adenauer Foundation, 2001.

American University in Cairo, Social Research Center. "Economic Participation of Women in Egypt: A Resource Site on the Employment of Women in Egypt." <http://www.aucegypt.edu/src/wsite1/index.htm>

Amin, Ruhul, Jamir Chowdhury, Ashraf U. Ahmed, M. Ahmed. "Poor Women's Participation in Income-Generating Projects and Their Fertility Regulation in Rural Bangladesh: Evidence From a Recent Survey," *World Development* 22, no.4 (April 1994):555–66. Accessed through Proquest.

Amin, Sajeda, Ian Diamond, Ruchira T. Naved, Margaret Newby. "Transition to Adulthood of Female Garment-Factory Workers in Bangladesh," *Studies in Family Planning* 29, no. 2 (June 1998): 185–201.

Amirthalingam, Kumaralingam. "Women's Rights, International Norms, and Domestic Violence: Asian Perspectives," *Human Rights Quarterly* 27, no. 2 (May 2005): 683–710.

Ammar, Nawal, and Leila Lababidy. "Women's Grassroots Movements and Democratization in Egypt." In Bystyzienski and Sekhon, eds., *Democratization and Women's Grassroots Movements*. Bloomington: Indiana University Press, 1998.

Anderson, Nancy Fix. "Benazir Bhutto and Dynastic Politics: Her Father's Daughter, Her People's Sister." In Michael A. Genovese, ed., *Women as National Leaders*. Newbury Park, CA: Sage, 1993.

An-Naim, Abdullahi. *Islamic Family Law in a Changing World: A Global Resource Book.* London: Zed Books, 2002.

Arat, Yesim. *The Patriarchal Paradox: Women Politicians in Turkey.* Rutherford, NJ: Fairleigh Dickinson University Press, 1989.

Arat, Yesim. *Rethinking Islam and Liberal Democracy: Islamist Women in Turkish Politics.* Albany: State University of New York Press, 2005.

Arat, Yesim. "A Woman Prime Minister in Turkey: Did It Matter," *Women and Politics* 19, no. 4 (Fall 1998): 1–22.

Arat, Zehra F. *Deconstructing Images of "The Turkish Woman."* New York: St. Martin's Press, 1998.

Arin, Canan Arin. "Women's Legal Status in Turkey." In Homa Hoodfar, ed., *Shifting Boundaries in Marriage and Divorce in Muslim Communities.* Montpelier, France: Women Living Under Muslim Laws, 1996.

Ask, Karin, and Marit Tjomsland. *Women and Islamization: Contemporary Dimensions of Discourse on Gender Relations.* Oxford: Berg Press 1998.

Assaad, Ragui and Fatma El-Hamidi. "Is All Work the Same? A Comparison of the Determinants of Female Participation and Hours of Work in Various Employment States in Egypt." In Mine Cinar, ed., *The Economics of Women and Work in the Middle East and North Africa.* Amsterdam: JAI Press, 2001.

Awn, Peter J. "Indian Islam: The Shah Bano Affair." In John Stratton Hawley, ed., *Fundamentalism and Gender.* New York: Oxford University Press, 1994.

Badran, Margot. "Between Secular and Islamic Feminism/s: Reflections on the Middle East and Beyond," *Journal of Middle East Women's Studies* 1, no. 1 (Winter 2005): 6–29.

Badran, Margot. *Feminists, Islam, and Nation: Gender and the Making of Modern Egypt.* Princeton: Princeton University Press, 1995.

Badran, Margot. "Toward Islamic Feminisms: A Look at the Middle East," 159–88. In *Hermeneutics of Honor: Negotiating Female "Public" Space in Islamic/ate Societies*, ed. Asma Afsaruddin. Cambridge, MA: Harvard University, Center for Middle Eastern Studies, 1999.

Badran, Margot, and Miriam Cooke, eds. *Opening the Gates: An Anthology of Arab Feminist Writing*, 2nd ed. Bloomington: Indiana University Press, 2004.

Bahramitash, Roksana. "Islamic Fundamentalism and Women's Economic Role: The Case of Iran," *International Journal of Politics, Culture, and Society* 16, no. 4 (2003): 551–68.

Bangasser, Paul. "The ILO and the Informal Sector: An Institutional History." Geneva: ILO, 2000. <http://www.ilo.org/public/english/employment/strat/publ/ep00-9.htm#Introduction>

Bara-Acal, Amer M., and Abdulmajid J. Astih. *Muslim Law on Personal Status in the Phillipines.* Quezon City, Phillipines: Central Professional Books, 1998.

Barazangi, Nimat, "Parents and Youth: Perceiving and Practicing Islam in North America." In Barbara C. Aswad and Barbara Bilgé, eds., *Family and Gender Among American Muslims: Issues Facing Middle Eastern Immigrants and Their Descendants.* Philadelphia: Temple University Press, 1996.

Barlas, Asma. *"Believing Women" in Islam: Unreading Patriarchal Interpretations of the Qur'an.* Austin: University of Texas Press, 2002.

Baron, Beth. "Unveiling in Early Twentieth-Century Egypt: Practical and Symbolic Considerations," *Middle Eastern Studies* 25, no. 3 (July 1989).

Bates, Lisa M. Sidney Ruth Schuler, Farzana Islam, Md Khairul Islam. "Socioeconomic Factors and Processes Associated with Domestic Violence in Rural Bangladesh," *International Family Planning Perspectives* 30, no. 4 (December 2004): 190–99.

Berik, Günseli. "Towards and Understanding of Gender Hierarchy in Turkey: A Comparative Analysis of Carpet-Weaving Villages in Turkey." In Sirin Tekeli, ed., *Women In Turkish Society.* London: Zed Books, 1995.

Bhatnagar, J. P. *Commentary on the Muslim Women: Containing the Muslim Women (Protection of Rights on Divorce) Act, 1986, the Muslim Women (Protection of Rights on Divorce) Rules, 1986, Maintenance, Etc., Etc.* Allahabad: Ashoka Law House, 1992.

Bibars, Iman. *Victims and Heroines: Women, Welfare and the Egyptian State.* London: Zed Books, 2001.

Bodman, Herbert L., and Nayereh Esfahlani Tohidi, eds. *Women in Muslim Societies: Diversity Within Unity.* Boulder: Lynne Rienner, 1998.

Bolak, Hale Cihan. "When Wives are Major Providers: Culture, Gender, and Family Work," *Gender and Society* 11, no.4 (August 1997): 409–33.

Bolak, Hale Cihan. "Towards a Conceptualization of Marital Power Dynamics: Women Breadwinners and Working Class Households in Turkey." In Sirin Tekeli, ed., *Women In Turkish Society.* London: Zed Books, 1995.

Bowen, Donna Lee. "Abortion, Islam and the 1994 Cairo Population Conference," *International Journal of Middle East Studies* 29, no. 2 (May 1997): 161–84.

Boris, Eileen and Elisabeth Prügl, eds. *Homeworkers in Global Perspective: Invisible No More*. New York: Routledge, 1996.

Bowen, Donna Lee and Evelyn A Early, eds. *Everyday Life in the Muslim Middle East*. Bloomington: Indiana University Press, 2002.

Boyle, Elizabeth. *Female Genital Cutting: Cultural Conflict in the International Community*. Baltimore: Johns Hopkins University Press, 2002.

Bahramitash, Roksana. "Globalization, Islamization, and Women's Employment in Indonesia." In Mary Ann Tétreault and Robert A. Denemark, eds., *Gods, Guns, and Globalization: Religious Radicalism and International Political Economy*. Boulder: Lynne Rienner, 2004.

Bahramitash, Roksana. "Islamic Fundamentalism and Women's Economic Role: The Case of Iran," *International Journal of Politics, Culture, and Society* 16, no. 4 (2003): 551–68.

Cachalia, Firoz. *The Future of Muslim Family Law in South Africa*. London: Centre for Applied Legal Studies; and Johannesburg: University of the Witwatersrand,. South African Constitutional Studies Centre, Institute of Commonwealth Studies, 1991.

Caldwell, John C. *Theory of Fertility Decline*. London: Academic Press, 1982.

Çağatay, Nilüfer, and Yasemin Nuhoğlu Soysal. "Comparative Observations on Feminism and the Nation-Building Process." In Sirin Tekeli, ed., *Women In Turkish Society*. London: Zed Books, 1995.

Charrad, Mounira, M. "Cultural Diversity Within Islam: Veils and Laws in Tunisia." In Herbert L. Bodman, and Nayereh Tohidi, eds., *Women in Muslim Societies: Diversity Within Unity* Boulder: Lynne Reiner, 1998.

Charrad, Mounira M. *States and Women's Rights: The Making of Postcolonial Tunisia, Algeria, and Morocco*. Berkeley: University of California Press, 2001.

Chatty, Dawn. *Mobile Pastoralists: Development Planning and Social Change in Oman*. New York: Columbia University Press, 1996.

Chatty, Dawn, and Annika Rabo, eds. *Organizing Women: Formal and Informal Women's Groups in the Middle East*. Oxford: Berg, 1997.

Chatty, Dawn. "Women Working in Oman: Individual Choice and Cultural Constraints." In *International Journal of Middle East Studies* 32, no. 2 (May 2000): 241–54.

Cleveland, William. *A History of the Modern Middle East*. Boulder: Westview Press, 2000.

Cinar, Mine, ed. *The Economics of Women and Work in the Middle East and North Africa*. Amsterdam: JAI Press, 2001.

Cinar, E. Mine and Nejat Anbarci. "Working Women and Power Within Two-Income Turkish Households." In Mine Cinar, ed., *The Economics of Women and Work in the Middle East and North Africa*. Amsterdam: JAI Press, 2001.

Cindoglu, Dilek. "Virginity Tests and Artificial Virginity in Modern Turkish Medicine," *Women's Studies International Forum* 20, no. 2 (March 1997): 253–60.

Cooke, Miriam. *Women Claim Islam: Creating Islamic Feminism through Literature.* New York: Routledge, 2001.

Crotty, William, ed. *Democratic Development and Political Terrorism: The Global Perspective.* Boston: Northeastern University Press, 2005.

Cunningham, Karla. "Cross-Regional Trends in Female Terrorism," *Studies in Conflict & Terrorism* 26, no. 3 (2003): 171–96

Cunningham, Karla J. "Women, Political Violence, and Democratization." In William Crotty, ed. *Democratic Development and Political Terrorism: The Global Perspective.* Boston: Northeastern University Press, 2005.

Cwikel, Julie, Rachel Lev Wiesel, and Alean Al-Krenawi. "The Physical and Psychosocial Health of Bedouin Arab Women of the Negev Area of Israel: The Impact of High Fertility and Pervasive Domestic Violence," *Violence Against Women* 9, no. 2 (February 2003): 240–58.

Darrow, William R. "Marxism and Religion: Islam." In Charles Wei-hsun Fu and Gerhard E. Spiegler, eds., *Movements and Issues in World Religions: A Sourcebook and Analysis of Developments Since 1945.* Westport, CN: Greenwood Press, 1987.

DeLong-Bas, Natana. *Wahhabi Islam: From Revival and Reform to Global Jihad.* Oxford University Press, 2004.

Doumato, Eleanor Abdella. *Getting God's Ear: Women, Islam and Healing in Saudi Arabia and the Gulf.* New York: Columbia University Press, 2000.

Doumato, Eleanor Abdella. "Women and Work in Saudi Arabia: How Flexible are Islamic Margins?" *Middle East Journal* 53, no. 4 (Autumn 1999): 568–83.

Doumato, Eleanor Abdella and Marsha Pripstein Posusney, eds. *Women and Globalization in the Arab Middle East: Gender, Economy, and Society.* Boulder: Lynne Rienner, 2003.

Eickelman, Dale. "Anthropology, The Middle East & Central Asia." In Dale Eickelman, *The Middle East and Central Asia: An Anthropological Approach.* Upper Saddle River, NJ: Prentice Hall, 1998.

El Guindi, Fadwa. "Gendered Resistance, Feminist Veiling, Islamic Feminism." *Ahfad Journal* 22, no. 1 (June 2005): 53–79. Accessed through Proquest.

El Guindi, Fadwa. *Veil: Modesty, Privacy and Resistance*. Oxford, UK: Berg Publishers, 1999.

El-Laithy, Heba. *The Gender Dimensions of Poverty in Egypt*, 2000.
    <www.erf.org.eg/html/Heba_ElLaithy.pdf>

El-Sanabary, Nagat. "Women in Some Liberal Modernizing Islamic Countries." In Nelly P.
    Stromquist and Karen Monkman, eds., *Women in the Third World: An Encyclopedia of
    Contemporary Issues*. New York: Garland, 1998.

El Sadaawi, Nawal. *The Hidden Face of Eve: Women in the Arab World*. London: Zed, 1980.

England, Richard W., and Jonathan M. Harris. "Alternatives to Gross National Product: A
    Critical Survey." In Frank Ackerman, David Kiron, Neva Goodwin, Jonathan Harris, and
    Kevin P. Gallagher, eds., *Human Well-Being and Economic Goals*. Washington, DC:
    Island Press, 1998.

Erman, Tahire. "The Impact of Migration on Rural Women: Four Emergent Patterns," *Gender
    and Society* 12, no. 2 (April, 1998): 146–64.

Esfandiari, Haleh. *Reconstructed Lives: Women and Iran's Islamic Revolution*. Baltimore:
    Johns Hopkins University Press 1997.

Esim, Simel. "Why Women Earn Less? Gender-Based Factors Affecting the Earnings of Self-
    Employed Women in Turkey." In Mine Cinar, ed., *The Economics of Women and Work
    in the Middle East and North Africa*. Amsterdam: JAI Press, 2001.

Esim, Simel, and Eileen Kuttab. "Women's Informal Employment in Palestine: Securing a
    Livelihood Against All Odds." Working Paper 0213. Cairo, Egypt: Economic Research
    Forum, 2002.

Esposito, John L., with Natana J. DeLong-Bas. *Women in Muslim Family Law*. 2nd ed.
    Syracuse, NY: Syracuse University Press, 2001.

Fafchamps, Marcel, and Agnes R Quisumbing. "Social Roles, Human Capital, and the
    Intrahousehold Division of Labor: Evidence from Pakistan," *Oxford Economic Papers*
    55, no. 1 (January 2003): 36ff. Accessed through Proquest.

Farah, Nadia Ramsis. *Situation Analysis of Egyptian Rural Women and Women in Agriculture*.
    Cairo: UNFPA, 2001.

Fargues, Philippe. "Women in Arab Countries: Challenging the Patriarchal System?"
    Population et Sociétés 387 (February 2003).

Farsoun, Michael, Nadine Khoury, and Carol Underwood. "*In Their Own Words:* A Qualitative
    Study of Family Planning in Jordan," *Field Report*, no. 6 (October 1996).
    <http://www.jhuccp.org/pubs/fr/6/index.shtml>

Ferber, Marianne A., and Julie A. Nelson. *Beyond Economic Man: Feminist Theory and Economics*. Chicago: The University of Chicago Press, 1993.

Ferber, Marianne A., and Julie A. Nelson. *Feminist Economics Today: Beyond Economic Man*. Chicago: University of Chicago Press, 2003.

Ferree, Myra Marx, Shamus Khan, and Shauna A. Morimoto. "Assessing the Feminist Revolution: The Presence and Absence of Gender in Theory and Practice." June 25, 2005. < http://www.ssc.wisc.edu/~mferree/ferree%20khan%20morimoto%20-%20final.doc>

Fernea, Elizabeth Warnock. *In Search of Islamic Feminism: One Woman's Journey*. N.Y.: Doubleday, 1998.

Fernea, Elizabeth Warnock. *In Search of Islamic Feminism: One Woman's Global Journey*. New York: Bantam Books, 1998.

Fleischmann, Ellen L. *The Nation and Its "New" Women: The Palestinian Women's Movement, 1920-1948*. Berkeley: University of California Press, 2003.

Freedman, Robert. "Asia's Recent Fertility Decline and Prospects for Future Demographic Change," *Asia-Pacific Population Research Reports*, no. 1 (January 1995): 1–28.

Gallagher, Nancy. "Women's Human Rights on Trial in Jordan: The Triumph of Toujan al-Faisal," and Toujan al-Faisal, " They Insult Us and We Elect Them." In Mehnaz Afkami, ed., *Faith and Freedom: Women's Human Rights in the Muslim World*. Syracuse, NY: Syracuse University Press, 1995.

Gambetta, Diego, ed. *Making Sense of Suicide Missions*. Oxford: Oxford University Press, 2005.

Gani, H. A. *Reform of Muslim Personal Law: the Shah Bano Controversy and the Muslim Women (Protection of Rights on Divorce) Act, 1986*. New Delhi: Deep & Deep Publications, 1988.

Gardner, Katy. "Women and Islamic Revivalism in a Bangladeshi Community." In Patricia Jeffery and Amrita Basu, eds., *Appropriating Gender: Women's Activism and Politicized Religion in South Asia*. New York: Routledge, 1998.

Giacaman, Rita. *Palestinian Women: A Status Report*. Birzeit: Birziet University, 1997

Giacaman, Rita, and Penny Johnson, eds. *Inside Palestinian Households: Initial Analysis of a Community-Based Household Survey*. Birzeit: Institute of Women's Studies and Institute for Community and Public Health, Birzeit University, 2002.

Ghannam, Farha. *Remaking the Modern: Space, Relocation and the Politics of Identity in a Global Cairo*. Berkeley: University of California Press, 2002.

Ghavamshahidi, Zohreh. "'Bibi Khanum'." In Eileen Boris and Elisabeth Prügl, eds. *Homeworkers in Global Perspective: Invisible No More.* New York: Routledge, 1996.

Gole, Nilufer. *The Forbidden Modern: Civilization and Veiling.* Ann Arbor: University of Michigan Press; 1996.

Gray, Leslie, and Michael Kevane. "Diminished Access, Diverted Exclusion: Women and Land Tenure in Sub-Saharan Africa," *African Studies Review* 42, no. 2 (September 1999): 1–15. Accessed through Proquest.

Gruenbaum, Ellen. *The Female Circumcision Controversy: An Anthropological Perspective.* Philadelphia: University of Pennsylvania Press, 2001.

Gülük-Senesen, Gulay, and Semsa Özar. "Gender-Based Occupational Segregation in the Turkish Banking Sector." In Mine Cinar, ed., *The Economics of Women and Work in the Middle East and North Africa.* Amsterdam: JAI Press, 2001.

Haddad, Yvonne Yazbeck, and John L. Esposito, eds. *Islam, Gender, and Social Change.* New York: Oxford University Press, 1998.

Haddad, Yvonne Yazbeck, and John L. Esposito. *The Islamic Revival Since 1988: A Critical Survey and Bibliography.* Westport, CN: Greenwood Publishing, 1997.

Haddad, Yvonne Yazbeck, John Obert Voll, and John L. Esposito. *The Contemporary Revival: A Critical Survey and Bibliography.* New York: Greenwood Press, 1991.

Haeri, Shahla. *Law of Desire: Temporary Marriage in Shi'i Iran.* Syracuse, NY: Syracuse University Press, 1989.

Haeri, Shahla. "Women's Body, Nation's Honor: Rape in Pakistan." In Asma Afsaruddin, ed. *Hermeneutics and Honor: Negotiating Female "Public" Space in Islamic/ate Societies.* Cambridge, MA: Center for Middle Eastern Studies, Harvard University Press, 1999.

Hajjar, Lisa. "Domestic Violence and Sharia: A Comparative Study of Muslim Societies in the Middle East, Africa and Asia." <http://www.law.emory.edu/IFL/>

Hale, Sondra. *Gender Politics in Sudan: Islamism, Socialism, and the State.* Boulder: Westview Press, 1998.

Hallaq, Wael B. *The Origins and Evolution of Islamic Law.* Cambridge, UK: Cambridge University Press, 2005.

Hammami, Rema. "Gender Segmentation in the West Bank and Gaza Strip: Explaining the Absence of Palestinian Women from the Formal Labor Force." In Mine Cinar, ed., *The Economics of Women and Work in the Middle East and North Africa.* Amsterdam: JAI Press, 2001.

Hass, Amira. *Drinking the Sea at Gaza: Days and Nights in a Land Under Siege.* Trans., Elana Wesley, Maxine Kaufman Lacusta, Maxine Kaufman-Lacusta. New York: Owl Books, 2000.

Hassan, Riffat. "Equal Before Allah: Woman/Man Equality in the Islamic Tradition', *Harvard Divinity Bulletin 7*, no. 2 (Jan-May 1987).

Hassan, Sharifa Zaleha Syed, and Sven Cedrroth. *Managing Marital Disputes in Malaysia: Islamic Mediators and Conflict Resolution in the Syariah Courts.* Nordic Institute of Asian Studies Monograph Series, no. 75. Surrey, UK: Curzon Press, 1997.

Hassan, Yasmeen. *The Haven Becomes Hell: A Study of Domestic Violence in Pakistan.* Lahore: Shirkat Gah, 1995.

Hassan, Zoya, and Ritu Menon. *Unequal Citizens: A Study of Muslim Women in India.* New Delhi: Oxford University Press, 2004

Hassouneh-Phillips, Dean Saadat. "Marriage Is Half of Faith and the Rest Is Fear of Allah:" *Violence Against Women* 7, no. 8 (2001): 927–46.

Hatem, Mervat. "Modernization, the State, and the Family in Middle East Women's Studies," 63-87. In Margaret L. Meriwether and Judith E. Tucker, eds., *Social History of Women and Gender in the Modern Middle East.* Boulder: Westview Press, 1999.

Hatem, Mervat. "Secular and Islamist Discourses on Modernity in Egypt and Evolution of the Postcolonial Nation-State." In Yvonne Haddad and John L. Esposito, *Islam, Gender, and Social Change.* New York: Oxford University Press, 1998.

Hélie-Lucas, Marie-Aimée. "The Preferential Symbol for Islamic Identity: Women in Muslim Personal Laws," 391-407. In Valentine Moghadam, ed., *Identity Politics and Women: Cultural Reassertions and Feminisms in International Perspective.* Boulder: Westview Press, 1994.

Hessini, Leila. *From Uncivil War to Civil Peace: Algerian Women's Voices.* New York: Population Council, UNIFEM/AFWIC, 1998.

Hessini, Leila. *Living on a Fault Line: Political Violence Against Women in Algeria.* New York: Population Council, UNIFEM/AFWIC, 1996.

Hijab, Nadia, "Women and Work in the Arab World." In Suha Sabbagh, ed., *Arab Women: Between Defiance and Restraint.* New York: Olive Branch Press, 1997.

Hirsch, Susan F. *Pronouncing and Persevering: Gender and the Discourses of Disputing in an African Islamic Court.* Chicago: University of Chicago Press, 1998.

Hoffman-Ladd, Valerie J. "Polemics on the Modesty and Segregation of Women in Contemporary Egypt." In *International Journal of Middle East Studies* 19, no. 1 (1987): 23–50.

Hoodfar, Homa. *Between Marriage and the Market: Intimate Politics and Survival in Cairo.* Berkeley: University of California Press, 1997.

Hoodfar, Homa. "Circumventing Legal Limitation: Mahr and Marriage Negotiation in Egyptian Low Income Communities." Pages 121-42 in Homa Hoodfar, ed., *Shifting Boundaries in Marriage and Divorce in Muslim Communities.* Montpelier, France: Women Living Under Muslim Laws, 1996.

Hoodfar, Homa. "The Veil in Their Minds and on Our Heads: Veiling Practices and Muslim Women." Pages 248–79 in Lisa Lowe and David Lloyd, eds., *The Politics of Culture in the Shadow of Capital.* Durham, NC: Duke University Press, 1997.

Hoodfar, Homa, ed. *Shifting Boundaries in Marriage and Divorce in Muslim Communities.* Montpelier, France: Women Living Under Muslim Laws, 1996.

Hussain, Sabiha. "Do Women Really Have a Voice? Reproductive Behavior and Practices of Two Religious Communities," *Asian Journal of Women's Studies* 7, no. 4 (2001): 29–69.

Ibrahim, Saad Eddin. "Arab Social-Science Research in the 1990s and Beyond: Issues, Trends, and Priorities." Canada: International Development Research Centre. <http://www.idrc.ca/en/ev-41625-201-1-DO_TOPIC.html>

Inhorn, Marcia C. Quest for Conception: Gender, Infertility, and Egyptian Medical Traditions. Phladelphia: University of Pennsylvania Press, 1994.

Islamic Family Law. <http://www.law.emory.edu/IFL/>

Institute for Women's Studies in the Arab World. "Female Labor Force in Lebanon," *Al-Raida* 15, no. 82 (1998): 12–23.

International Labor Organization. *Estimates and Projections of the Economically Active Population, 1950–2010.* <http://www.ilo.org/public/english/bureau/stat/child/actrep/ecacpop.htm>

International Labor Organization. *Women and Men in the Informal Economy: A Statistical Picture.* Geneva: Employment Sector, 2002.

Interparliamentary Union. *Women in National Parliaments.* <http://www.ipu.org/wmn-e/classif.htm>

Interparliamentary Union. *Women's Suffrage: A World Chronology of Women's Rights to Vote and to Stand for Election.* <http://www.ipu.org/wmn-e/suffrage.htm>

Jai, Janak Raj, ed., *Shah Bano.* New Delhi: Rajiv, 1986.

James, Stanlie, and Claire Robertson, eds. *Genital Cutting and the Transnational Sisterhood.* Urbana: University of Illinois Press, 2002.

Jawad, Haifaa. *The Rights of Women in Islam: An Authentic Approach.* New York: MacMillan Press, 1998.

Jayawardena, Kumari. *Feminism and Nationalism in the Third World.* New Delhi: Kali for Women, 1986.

Jeffery, Patricia, and Amrita Basu, eds. *Appropriating Gender: Women's Activism and Politicized Religion in South Asia.* New York: Routledge, 1998.

Jones, Gavin W. "The Changing Indonesian Household." In Kathryn Robinson and Sharon Bessell, eds., *Women in Indonesia: Gender, Equity, and Development.* Singapore: Institute of Southeast Asian Studies, 2002.

Jones, Gavin W. *Marriage and Divorce in Islamic South-East Asia* (Kuala Lumpur: Oxford University Press, 1994.

Jones, Gavin W., and Mehtab S. Karim, eds. *Islam, the State and Population.* Karachi: Oxford University Press, 2005.

Jones, Jennifer. "Around the Globe, Women Outlive Men," 2001, Population Reference Bureau Web site. <http://ww.prb.org>

Joseph, Saud. "Brother-Sister Relationships: Connectivity, Love and Power in the Reproduction of Patriarchy in Lebanon." In Suad Joseph, ed., *Intimate Selving in Arab Families: Gender, Self and Identity.* Syracuse, NY: Syracuse University Press, 1999.

Joseph, Suad. "Elite Strategies for State Building: Women, Family, Religion and the State in Iraq and Lebanon." In Deniz Kandiyoti, ed., *Women Islam and the State.* Hong Kong: Temple University Press, 1991.

Joseph, Suad. "Gender and Family in the Arab world." In Suha Sabbagh, ed., *Arab Women Between Defiance and Restraint.* New York: Olive Branch Press, 1996.

Joseph, Suad. "My Son/Myself, My Mother/Myself: Paradoxical Relationalities of Patriarchal Connectivity." In Suad Joseph, ed., *Intimate Selving in Arab Families: Gender, Self, and Identity.* Syracuse, NY: Syracuse University Press, 1999.

Joseph, Suad. "The Reproduction of Political Process Among Women Activists in Lebanon: Shopkeepers and Feminists." In Dawn Chatty and Annika Rabo, eds., *Organizing Women: Formal and Informal Women's Groups in the Middle East.* Oxford: Berg, 1997.

Joseph, Suad. "Straddling Visible and Invisible Lebanese Economies." In Richard Lobban, Jr., ed., *Middle Eastern Women and The Invisible Economy.* Gainesville, FL: University of Florida Press, 1998.

Joseph, Suad. "Women and Politics in the Middle East." In Suad Joseph and Susan Slyomovics, eds. *Women and Power in the Middle East.* Philadelphia, PA: University of Pennsylvania Press, 2001.

Joseph, Suad, ed. *Gender and Citizenship in the Middle East.* Syracuse, NY: Syracuse University Press, 2000.

Joseph, Suad, ed. *Intimate Selving in Arab Families; Gender, Self, and Identity.* Syracuse, NY: Syracuse University Press, 1999.

Joseph, Suad, et al., ed. *Encyclopedia of Women and Islamic Cultures: Methodologies, Paradigms, and Sources* I. Leiden, Netherlands: Brill, 2003.

Joseph, Suad, and Susan Slyomovics, eds. *Women and Power in the Middle East.* Philadelphia, PA: University of Pennsylvania Press, 2001.

Kabasakal, Hayat. "A Profile of Top Managers in Turkey," in Zehra Arat, *Deconstructing Images of "The Turkish Woman."* New York: St. Martin's Press, 1998.

Kabeer, Naila. *The Power to Choose: Bangladeshi Women and Labour Market Decisions in London and Dhaka.* London: VERSO, 2000.

Kabeer, Naila. *"We Don't Do Credit": Nijera Kori, Social Mobilisation and the Collective Capabilities of the Poor in Rural Bangladesh.* Dhaka, Bangladesh: Nijera Kori, 2002.

Kamalkhani, Zehra. *Women's Islam: Religious Practice among Women in Today's Iran.* London: Kegan Paul International, 1998.

Kanaaneh, Rhoda. *Birthing the Nation: Strategies of Palestinian Women in Israel.* Berkeley: University of California Press, 2002.

Kandiyoti, Deniz. "Bargaining With Patriarchy," *Gender and Society* 2, no. 3 (September 1988): 274–90.

Kandiyoti, Deniz. "Contemporary Feminist Scholarship and Middle East Studies," in Deniz Kandiyoti, ed., *Gendering the Middle East: Emerging Perspectives.* Syracuse, NY: Syracuse University Press, 1996.

Kandiyoti, Deniz. " Household Surveys in Post-Soviet Central Asia." In S. Razavi, ed., *Gendered Poverty and Well-Being.* Oxford: Blackwell Publishers, 2000.

Kandiyoti, Deniz. "Islam and Patriarchy: A Comparative Perspective." In Keddie and Baron, eds., *Shifting Boundaries.*

Kandiyoti, Deniz. "The Politics of Gender and the Conundrums of Citizenship." In Suad Joseph and Susan Slyomovics, eds., *Women and Power in the Middle East.* Philadelphia: University of Pennsylvania Press, 2001.

Kandiyoti, Deniz, ed. *Gendering the Middle East: Emerging Perspectives.* Syracuse: Syracuse University Press, 1996.

Kandiyoti, Deniz, ed. *Women, Islam, and the State.* Philadelphia: Temple University Press, 1991.

Kaplan, Caren, Norma Alarcón, and Minoo Moallem, ed. *Between Woman and Nation: Nationalisms, Transnational Feminisms and the State.* Durham, NC: Duke University Press, 1999.

Karam, Azza. *Women, Islamisms and State: Contemporary Feminisms in Egypt.* London and New York: Macmillan and St. Martin's Press, 1998.

Karshenas, Massoud, and Valentine M. Moghadam. "Female Labor Force Participation and Economic Adjustment in the MENA Region." In Mine Cinar, ed., *The Economics of Women and Work in the Middle East and North Africa.* Amsterdam, Netherlands: JAI Press, 2001.

Keddie, Nikki. "The Study of Muslim Women in the Middle East: Achievements and Remaining Problems," *Harvard Middle Eastern and Islamic Review* 6 (2000): 26–52.

Keddie, Nikki. "Women in the Limelight: Some Recent Books on Middle Eastern Women's History," *International Journal of Middle East Studies* 34, no. 3 (2002): 553–73

Keddie, Nikki R., and Beth Baron, eds. *Women in Middle Eastern History: Shifting Boundaries in Sex and Gender.* New Haven: Yale University Press, 1991.

Khan, Muniza Rafiq. *Socio-Legal Status of Muslim Women.* New Delhi and New York: Radian Advent Books, 1993.

Khan, Shahnaz. *Muslim Women Crafting a North American Identity.* Gainesville, FL: University Press of Florida, 2000.

Khoury, Nabil F., and Valentine M. Moghadam, eds. *Gender and Development in the Arab World: Women's Economic Participation: Patterns and Policies.* Tokyo: Zed Books and United Nations University Press, 1995.

Layish, Aharon. "Contributions of the Modernists to the Secularization of Islamic Law," *Middle Eastern Studies* 14 (1978).

Layish, Aharon. *Divorce in the Libyan Family: A Study Based on the Sijjls of the Shari'a Courts of Ajdabiyya and Kufra.* New York: New York University Press, 1991.

Lobban, Richard A., ed. *Middle Eastern Women and The Invisible Economy.* Gainesville, FL: University of Florida Press, 1998.

Lowe, Lisa, and David Lloyd, eds. *The Politics of Culture in the Shadow of Capital.* Durham, NC: Duke University Press, 1997.

Macleod, Arlene Elowe. *Accommodating Protest: Working Women, The New Veiling, and Change in Cairo.* New York: Columbia University Press, 1991.

Mahmood, Syed Tahir. *Statutes of Personal Law in Islamic Countries: History, Texts, and Analysis*. 2nd rev. ed. New Delhi: India and Islam Research Council, 1995.

Marcus, Gill. "On Women in South Africa," August 8, 1997. <http://gos.sbc.edu/m/marcus.html>

Mason, Andrew, ed. *Population Change and Economic Development in East Asia: Challenges Met, Opportunities Seized*. Stanford: Contemporary Issues in Asia and the Pacific, Stanford University Press, 2001. Available online at <http://www.sup.org>

Matin, Abdul. *Bangladesh: The Muslim Personal Laws*. Dhaka: Palok Publishers, 1989.

Meriwether, Margaret L., and Judith E. Tucker, eds. *Social History of Women and Gender in the Modern Middle East*. Boulder: Westview Press, 1999.

Mernissi, Fatima. *Beyond the Veil: Male-Female Dynamics in Modern Muslim Society*. Rev. ed. Bloomington: Indiana University Press, 1987.

Mernissi, Fatima, *The Veil and the Male Elite: A Feminist Interpretation of Women's Rights in Islam*. Reading, MA: Addison-Wesley, 1991.

Mernissi, Fatima. *Women and Islam: An Historical and Theological Enquiry*. Trans. by Mary Jo Lakeland. Oxford: Blackwell, 1991.

Mernissi, Fatima. *Women's Rebellion and Islamic Memory*. London: Zed Books, 1996.

Messaoudi, Khalida. *Unbowed: An Algerian Woman Confronts Islamic Fundamentalism: Interviews with Elizabeth Schemla*. Trans., Anne C. Vila. Philadelphia, PA: University of Pennsylvania Press 1998.

Miller, Carol, and Jessica Vivian. *Women's Employment in the Textile Manufacturing Sectors of Bangladesh and Morocco*. Geneva: UNRISD in cooperation with UNDP, 2002.

Mir-Hosseini, Ziba. *Islam and Gender: The Religious Debate in Contemporary Iran*. Princeton, NJ: Princeton University Press, 1999.

Mir-Hosseini, Ziba. *Marriage on Trial: Islamic Family Law in Iran and Morocco*. London: I. B. Taurus, 2000.

Moaddel, Mansoor, and Taghi Azadarmaki. "The Worldviews of Islamic Publics: The Cases of Egypt, Iran, and Jordan," *Comparative Sociology* 1, nos. 3-4 (2002): 299–319.

Moghissi, Haideh. *Feminism and Islamic Fundamentalism: The Limits of Postmodern Analysis*. London: Zed, 1999.

Moghissi, Haideh. *Populism and Feminism in Iran: Women's Struggle in a Male-Defined Revolutionary Movement*. New York: St. Martin's, 1996.

Moghissi, Haideh. "Women in the Resistance Movement in Iran." In Haleh Afshar, ed., *Women in the Middle East: Perceptions, Realities, and Struggles for Liberation.* New York: St. Martin's, 1993.

Moghissi, Haideh. "Women, Modernity, and Political Islam." *Iran Bulletin* 19–20 (Autumn/Winter 1998): 42–44.

Moghadam, Valentine M. *Globalizing Women: Transnational Feminist Networks.* Baltimore: Johns Hopkins University Press, 2005.

Moghadam, Valentine M. "Islamic Feminism and Its Discontents: Toward a Resolution of of the Debate," *Signs* 27, no. 4 (Summer 2002): 1135–72.

Moghadam, Valentine M. *Modernizing Women: Gender and Social Change in the Middle East.* 2nd ed. Boulder: Lynne Rienner, 2003.

Moghadam, Valentine M. "Patriarchy in Transition: Women and the Changing Family in the Middle East." *Journal of Comparative Family Studies* 35, no. 2 (Spring 2004): 137–63.

Moghadam, Valentine M. "Transnational Feminist Networks: Collective Action in an Era of Globalization," *International Sociology* 15, no. 1 (2000): 57–84.

Moghadam, Valentine M. "Women's Economic Participation in the Middle East: What Difference has the Neoliberal Policy Turn Made?" *Journal of Middle East Women's Studies* 1, no. 1 (2004): 110–46.

Moghadam, Valentine. M. Women's NGO's in the Middle East and North Africa: Constraints, Opportunities, and Priorities." In Dawn Chatty and A. Rabo, eds., *Organizing Women: Formal and Informal Women's Groups in the Middle East.* Oxford: Berg, 1997.

Moghadam, Valentine M. *Women, Work, and Economic Reform in the Middle East and North Africa.* Boulder: Lynne Rienner, 1998.

Moghadam, Valentine M. "Women, Work, and Economic Restructuring: A Regional Overview." In Mine Cinar, ed., *The Economics of Women and Work in the Middle East and North Africa.* Amsterdam: JAI Press, 2001.

Moghadam, Valentine M., ed. *Gender and National Identity: Women and Politics in Muslim Society.* London: Zed Books, 1994.

Mohanty, Chandra Talpate. "Under Western Eyes: Feminist Scholarship and Colonial Discourses." Pages 51-80 in Chandra Talpate Mohanty, et al., eds., *Third World Women and the Politics of Memory.* Bloomington: Indiana University Press, 1991.

Mojab, Shahrzad, and Nahla Abdo, eds. *Violence in the Name of Honour: Theoretical and Political Challenges.* Istanbul: Istanbul Bilgi Üniversitesi Yayinlari, 2004.

Molyneux, Maxine. "The Law, the State, and Socialist Policies with Regard to Women: The Case of the People's Democratic Republic of Yemen, 1967-1990." Pages 237–72 in Deniz Kandiyoti, ed., *Women, Islam and State.* Philadelphia: Temple University Press, 1991.

Monshipouri, Mahmood. "The Road to Globalization Runs Through Women's Struggle: Iran and the Impact of the Nobel Peace Prize," *World Affairs* 167, no. 1 (Summer 2004): 3–15.

Moore, Kathleen. "The *Hijab* and Religious Liberty: Anti-Discrimination Law and Muslim Women in the United States." In Yvonne Yazbeck Haddad and John L. Espostio, eds., *Muslims on the Americanization Path?* Oxford: Oxford University Press, 2000.

Moors, Annelies Moors. "Debating Islamic Family Law: Legal Texts and Social Practices." Pages 141–75" in Margaret L. Meriwether and Judith E. Tucker, eds., *Social History of Women and Gender in the Modern Middle East.* Boulder: Westview Press, 1999.

Moors, Annelies. *Women, Property and Islam: Palestinian Experiences 1920-1990.* Cambridge, UK: Cambridge University Press, 1995.

Morgan, S. Philip, Sharon Stash, Herbert L. Smith, and Karen Oppenheim Mason. "Muslim and Non-Muslim Differences in Female Autonomy and Fertility: Evidence from Four Asian Countries," *Population and Development Review* 28, no. 3 (2002): 515–37.

Mughni, Haya. *Women in Kuwait: the Politics of Gender.* London: Saqi Books, 2001.

Mukhopadhyay, Swapna, and Ratna M. Sudarshan Kali. "Tracking Gender Equity Under Economic Reforms: Continuity and Change in South Asia," 2003. <http://www.idrc.ca/uploads/user-S/Press/IDRC2004>

Mumtaz, Khawar. "Political Participation: Women in National Legislatures in Pakistan," 319–69. In Farida Shaheed, ed, *Shaping Women's Lives: Laws, Practices, and Strategies in Pakistan: Laws, Practices and Strategies in Pakistan.* Lahore: Shirkat Gah, Women's Resource Centre, 1998.

Musallam, Basim. "Contraception and the Rights of Women." Pages 29–38 in *Sex and Society in Islam: Birth Control Before the Nineteenth Century.* Cambridge, UK: Cambridge University Press, 1983.

Nachtwey, Jodi. "Explaining Women's Support for Political Islam: Contributions from Feminist Theory." Pages 48–69 in Mark Tessler, with Jodi Nachtwey and Anne Banda,eds., *Area Studies and Social Science: Strategies for Understanding Middle East Politics.* Bloomington: Indiana University Press, 1999.

Najmabadi, Afsaneh. "Crafting an Educated Housewife in Iran." In Lila Abu-Lughod, ed., *Remaking Women: Feminism and Modernity in the Middle East.* Princeton: Princeton University Press, 1998.

Najmabadi, Afsaneh. "Feminism in an Islamic Republic: Years of Hardship, Years of Growth." In Yvonne Yazbeck Haddad and John L. Esposito Islam, eds., *Gender, and Social Change*. New York: Oxford University Press, 1998.

Najmabadi, Afsaneh. "Hazards of Modernity and Morality: Women, State, and Ideology in Contemporary Iran." Pages 48–77 in Kandiyoti, ed., *Women, Islam and State*.

Nashat, Guity, and Judith Tucker. *Women in the Middle East and North Africa*. Bloomington: Indiana University Press 1998.

Nasir, Jamal J. *The Islamic Law of Personal Status*. 3rd ed. New York: Kluwer Law International, 2002.

Nelson, Julie. *Feminism, Objectivity and Economics*. London: Routledge, 1996.

Nordquist, Joan ed. *Third World Women and Development*: *A Bibliography*. Santa Cruz, CA: Reference and Research Services, 2001.

Oey-Gardiner, Mayling. "And the Winner Is . . . Indonesian Women in Public Life." In Kathryn Robinson and Sharon Bessell, eds., *Women in Indonesia: Gender, Equity, and Development*. Singapore: Institute of Southeast Asian Studies, 2002.

Okten, Aysenur. "Post-Fordist Work, Political Islam and Women in Urban Turkey." In Mine Cinar, ed., *The Economics of Women and Work in the Middle East and North Africa*. Amsterdam: JAI Press, 2001.

Olmsted, Jennifer C. "Is Paid Work The (Only) Answer? Neoliberalism, Arab Women's Well-Being, and the Social Contract," *Journal of Middle East Women's Studies* 1, no. 2 (Spring 2005): 112–41.

Olmsted, Jennifer. "Men's Work/Women's Work: Employment, Wages and Occupational Segregation in Bethlehem." In Mine Cinar, ed., *The Economics of Women and Work in the Middle East and North Africa*. Amsterdam: JAI Press, 2001.

Olmsted, Jennifer. "Reexamining the Fertility Puzzle in the Middle East and North Africa." In Eleanor Doumato and Marsha Pripstein-Posusney, eds., *Women and Globalization in the Arab Middle East: Gender, Economy and Society*. Boulder: Lynne Rienner, 2003.

Omran, Abdel Rahim. *Family Planning in the Legacy of Islam*. New York: Routledge, 1992.

Özar, Semsa, and Gulay Gülük-Senesen. "Determinants of Female (Non-)Participation in the Urban Labor Force in Turkey," *METU Studies in Development* 25, no. 2 (1998): 311–28.

Parvin Paidar. Women and the Political Process in Twentieth-Century Iran. Cambridge: Cambridge University Press, 1995.

Parla, Ayse. "The 'Honor' of the State: Virginity Examinations in Turkey," *Feminist Studies*, 27, no. 1 (Spring 2001): 65–90.

Pearl, David S. *Islamic Family Law and Its Reception by the Courts in England.* Cambridge, MA: Islamic Legal Studies Program, 2000.

Phillips, James F., and Mian Bazle Hossain. *The Impact of Family Planning Household Service Delivery on Women's Status in Bangladesh*, no. 118, 1998. <http://www.popcouncil.org/pdfs/wp/118.pdf>

Quisumbing, Agnes R., and John A Maluccio. "Resources at Marriage and Intrahousehold Allocation: Evidence from Bangladesh, Ethiopia, Indonesia, and South Africa," *Oxford Bulletin of Economics and Statistics* 65, no. 3 (July 2003): 283ff. Accessed through Proquest.

Quisumbing, Agnes R., and Keijiro Otsuka, "Land Inheritance and Schooling in Matrilineal Societies: Evidence from Sumatra," *World Development* 29, no. 12 (December 2001): 2093ff. Accessed through Proquest.

Ramana, P.V.L. *Women in Slums: A Study of Women in a Muslim Slum of Visakhapatnam.* New Delhi: Serials Publications, 2002.

Rashad Hoda, and Magued Osman. "Nuptiality in Arab Countries: Changes and Implication." In Nicholas Hopkins, ed., *The New Arab Family.* Cairo Papers in Social Sciences 24, nos. 1–2. Cairo: The American University in Cairo Press, 2003.

Reid, Anthony. *Southeast Asia in the Age of Commerce 1450–1680*: Vol. 2, *Expansion and Crisis.* New Haven: Yale University Press, 1993.

Rispler-Chaim, Vardit. *Islamic Medical Ethics in the 20th Century.* New York: Brill, 1993.

Rispler-Chaim, Vardit. "The Right Not to Be Born: Abortion of the Disadvantaged Fetus in Contemporary Fatwas," *Muslim World* 89, no. 2 (1999).

Roald, Anne Sofie. *Women in Islam: The Western Experience.* New York: Routledge, 2001.

Robinson, Kathryn, and Sharon Bessell, eds. *Women in Indonesia: Gender, Equity, and Development.* Singapore: Institute of Southeast Asian Studies, 2002.

Rogers, T. "The Islamic Ethics of Abortion in the Traditional Islamic Sources." *Muslim World*, 89, no. 2 (1999): 122–29.

Roy, Olivier. *Globalized Islam: The Search for a New Ummah.* New York: Columbia University Press, 2004.

Rubenberg, Cheryl. *Palestinian Women: Patriarchy and Resistance in the West Bank.* Boulder: Lynn Rienner, 2001.

Rudi, N. *Selected Demographic Indicators of Arab Countries and Turkey.* Washington, DC: Population Reference Bureau, 2001. <http://www.prb.org>

Sabbagh, Suha, ed. *Arab Women: Between Defiance and Restraint.* New York: Olive Branch Press, 1997.

Sabbagh, Suha, ed. *Palestinian Women of Gaza and the West Bank.* Bloomington: Indiana University Press, 1998.

Safi, Omid, ed. *Progressive Muslims on Justice, Gender, and Pluralism.* Oxford: Oneworld, 2003.

Saliba, Therese, Carolyn Allen, and Judith A. Howard, eds. *Gender, Politics, and Islam.* Chicago: University of Chicago Press, 2002.

Satchedina, A. " Woman, Half-the-Man? Crisis of Male Epistemology in Islamic Jurisprudence." In R.S. Khare, ed., *Perspectives on Islamic Law and Society.* Lanham, MD: Rowman & Littlefield, 1999.

Shah. Nik Noriani Nik Badli. *Marriage and Divorce: Law Reform Within Islamic Framework.* Kuala Lumpur: International Law Book Services, Golden Books Centre, 2000.

Shaheed, Farida, Asma Zia, and Sohail Warraich. *Women in Politics: Participation and Representation in Pakistan.* Lahore: Shirkat Gah, 1998.

Shaheed, Farida, Sohail Akbar Warraich, Cassandra Balchim, and Aisha Gazdar, eds. *Shaping Women's Lives: Laws, Practices and Strategies in Pakistan.* Lahore: Shirkat Gah, Women's Resource Centre, 1998.

Shahidian, Hammed. *Women in Iran: Gender Politics in the Islamic Republic.* Westport, CT: Greenwood Press, 2003.

Shalhoub-Kevorkian, Nadera. "Liberating Voices: The Political Implications of Palestinian Mothers Narrating Their Loss," *Women's Studies International Forum* 26, no. 5 (2003): 391–407. <http://womens-studies.syr.edu/Womens-Studies/CourseReader/OnlineReader/EGMethfemPalestinemoth.pdf>

Shami, Seteney, and Linda Herera, eds. *Between Field and Text: Emerging Voices in Egyptian Social Science.* Cairo: American University in Cairo Press, 1999.

Sharoni, Simona. *Gender and the Israeli-Palestinian Conflict: the Politics of Women's Resistance.* Syracuse, NY: Syracuse University Press 1995.

Sharabi, Hisham. *Neopatriarchy: A Theory of Distorted Change in Arab Society.* New York: Oxford University Press, 1988.

Shehabuddin, Elora. "Contesting the Illicit: Gender and the Politics of Fatwas in Bangladesh." Pages 161–200 in Therese Saliba, Carolyn Allen, and Judith A. Howard, eds., *Gender, Politics, and Islam.* Chicago: University of Chicago Press, 2002.

Shehadeh, Lamia Rustum, ed. *Women and War in Lebanon*. Gainesville, FL: University Press of Florida, 1999.

Shell-Duncan, Bettina, and Yvla Hernlund, eds. *Female "Circumcision" in Africa: Culture, Controversy and Change*. Boulder: Lynne Reiner, 2000.

Sholkamy, Hania. "Procreation in Islam: A Reading From Egypt of People and Texts." Pages 130–61 in Peter Loizos and Patrick Heady, eds., *Conceiving Persons: Ethnographies of Procreation, Fertility, and Growth*. New Brunswick, NJ: Athlone Press, 1999.

Shukri, Shirin J.A. *Arab Women: Unequal Partners in Development*. Aldershot, Hants, England: Avebury, 1996.

Shukri, Shirin J.A. *Social Changes and Women in the Middle East: State Policy, Education, Economics, and Development*. Aldershot, Hants, England: Ashgate, 1999.

Siapno, Jacqueline Aquino. *Gender, Islam, Nationalism, and the State in Aceh: The Paradox of Power, Co-optation, and Resistance*. London: Curzon Routledge, 2002.

Singerman, Diane. *Avenues of Participation: Family, Politics, and Networks in Urban Quarters of Cairo*. Princeton: Princeton University Press, 1995.

Singerman, Diane, and Homa Hoodfar. *Development, Change, and Gender in Cairo: A View from the Household*. Bloomington: Indiana University Press, 1996.

Skaine, Rosemarie. *The Women of Afghanistan Under the Taliban*. Jefferson, NC: McFarland, 2002.

Sleboda, Jennifer. "Islam and Women's Rights Advocacy in Malaysia," *Asian Journal of Women's Studies* 7, no. 2 (June 30, 2001): 94.

Sonbol, Amira El-Azhary. *Women of Jordan: Islam, Labor and the Law*. Syracuse, NY: Syracuse University Press, 2003.

Sonbol, Amira El-Azhary, ed. *Women, Family, and Divorce Laws*. Syracuse, NY: Syracuse University Press, 1996.

Stivens, Maila. *Matriliny and Modernity: Sexual Politics and Social Change in Rural Malaysia* Sydney: Allen and Unwin, 1996.

Stivens, Maila. "(Re)framing Women's Rights Claims in Malaysia." In Virginia Hooker and Noraini Othman, eds., *Malaysia, Islam, Society, and Politics: Essays in Honour of Clive S. Kessler*. Singapore: Institute of Southeast Asian Studies, 2003.

Stowasser, Barbara. "Gender Issues in Contemporary Qur'anic Interpretation." Pages 30–44 in Yvonne Yazbeck Haddad, and John L. Esposito, eds., *Islam, Gender, and Social Change*. New York: Oxford University Press, 1998.

Stowasser, Barbara. *Women in the Qur'an, Traditions, and Interpretation.* Oxford: Oxford University Press, 1996.

Stromquist, Nelly P., and Karen Monkman, eds. *Women in the Third World: An Encyclopedia of Contemporary Issues.* New York: Garland, 1998.

Sudqi, Dawoud El-Alami, and Doreen Hinchcliffe. *Islamic Marriage and Divorce Laws of the Arab World.* London and Boston: Kluwer Law International, 1996.

Susilastuti, Dewi Haryani. "Home-Based Work as a Rural Survival Strategy: A Central Javanese Perspective." In Eileen Boris and Elisabeth Prügl, eds., *Homeworkers in Global Perspective: Invisible No More.* New York: Routledge, 1996.

Taecker, Kevin R. "Myths and Realities About Unemployment in Saudi Arabia," *Saudi-American Forum Essay* 11 (March 30, 2003). Accessed online at www.saudi-american-forum.org/Newsletters/SAF_Essay_11.htm, on April 1, 2003.

Talatoff, Kamran. "Iranian Women's Literature: From Pre-Revolutionary Social Discourse to Post-Revolutionary Feminism," *International Journal of Middle East Studies* 29, no. 4: 531–58.

Tanzil-ur-Rahman. *Muslim Family Laws Ordinance: Islamic and Social Survey.* Karachi: Royal Book Company; 1997.

Tekeli, Sirin, ed. *Women In Turkish Society.* London: Zed Books, 1995.

Tessler, Mark, with Jodi Nachtwey and Anne Banda, eds. *Area Studies and Social Science: Strategies for Understanding Middle East Politics.* Bloomington: Indiana University Press, 1999.

Tétreault, Mary Ann, "Civil Society in Kuwait: Protected Spaces and Women's Rights," *Middle East Journal* 47, no. 2 (Spring 1993): 275–91.

Tétreault, Mary Ann, and Robert A. Denemark. *Gods, Guns, and Globalization: Religious Radicalism and International Political Economy.* Boulder: Lynne Rienner, 2004.

Tohidi, Nayereh. "Fundamentalist' Backlash and Muslim Women in the Beijing Conference: New Challenges for International Women's Movements," *Canadian Woman Studies* 16 no. 3 (Summer 1996b): 30–34.

Tohidi, Nayereh. "Gender and National Identity in Post-Soviet Azerbaijan: A Regional Perspective." Pages 249–92 in Ferida Acar and Ayse G. Ayata, eds., *Gender and Identity Construction: Women of Central Asia, the Caucasus and Turkey.* Boston: Brill, 2000.

Tohidi, Nayereh. "The Global-Local Intersection of Feminism in Muslim Societies: The Cases of Iran and Azerbaijan." *Social Research* 69, no. 3 (Fall 2002): 851–89. Accessed through Proquest.

Tohidi, Nayereh. "Guardians of the Nation: Women, Islam, and the Soviet Modernization in Azerbaijan." In Herbert Bodman and Nayereh Tohidi, eds., *Women in Muslim Societies: Diversity within Unity*. Boulder: Lynne Rienner, 1998.

Tohidi, Nayereh. "International Connections of the Iranian Women's Movement." In Nikki Keddie and Rudi Matthee, eds., *Iran and the Surrounding World: Interactions in Culture and Cultural Politics*. Seattle: University of Washington Press, 2002: 205–31.

Tohidi, Nayereh. "Islamic Feminism: Perils and Promises," *Middle East Women's Studies Review* 16, nos. 3–4 (Winter 2002). <http://www.amews.org/review/reviewarticles/tohidi.htm>

Tohidi, Nayereh. "Modernity, Islamization, and Women in Iran." In Valentine Moghadam, ed. *Gender and National Identity: Women and Politics in Muslim Societies*. London: Oxford University Press, 1994.

Tohidi, Nayereh. "Soviet in Public, Azeri in Private: Gender, Islam, and Nationality in Soviet and Post-Soviet Azerbaijan," *Women's Studies International Forum* 19, nos. 1 and 2 (1996): 111–23.

Tohidi, Nayereh, and Jane H. Bayes. "Women Redefining Modernity and Religion in the Globalized Context," 17–60. In Jane H. Bayes and Nayereh Tohidi, eds., *Globalization, Gender and Religion*. New York: Palgrave, 2001.

Tucker, Judith E. *In the House of the Law: Gender and Islamic Law in Ottoman Syria and Palestine*. Berkeley: University of California Press, 1998.

Tucker, Judith E. *Women in Nineteenth-Century Egypt*. Cairo, Egypt: American University in Cairo Press, 1986.

Tzannatos, Zafiris. *Women and Labor Market Changes in the Global Economy: Growth Helps, Inequalities Hurt and Public Policy Matters*. Washington, DC: Social Protection Unit, Human Development Network, World Bank, April 1998.

UNICEF. "Early Marriage: Child Spouses," *Innocenti Digest*, no. 7, (March 2001). [Florence, Italy: United Nations Innocenti Research Centre]. <http://www.unicef-icdc.org/publications/pdf/digest7e.pdf>

United Nations, United Nations Development Programme (UNDP). *The Arab Human Development Report 2002*. New York: UNDP, 2002. <www.undp.org/rbas/ahdr/english.html>

United Nations, United Nations Development Programme (UNDP). *The Arab Human Development Report 2004*. New York: UNDP, 2004. <www.undp.org/rbas/ahdr/english.html>

United Nations, United Nations Development Programme, Arab Fund for Economic and Social Development, and Arab Gulf Programme for United Nations Development Organization,

Arab Development Report 2004: Towards Freedom in the Arab World. New York: UNDP, 2004. <www.undp.org/ rbas/ahdr/english.html>

United Nations, U.N. Development Fund for Women (UNIFEM). *Progress of Arab Women: One Paradigm, Four Arenas, and more than 140 Million Women*, 2004. <http://www.arabwomenconnect.org/docs/PAW2004-beginning.pdf>

Urla-Zeytinoglu, Isik, et al. "Factors Affecting Female Managers' Careers in Turkey." In Mine Cinar, ed., *The Economics of Women and Work in the Middle East and North Africa.* Amsterdam: JAI Press, 2001.

Wadud, Amina. *Qur'an and Woman: Rereading the Sacred Text from a Woman's Perspective.* Oxford: Oxford University Press, 1999.

Wani, M. A. *Maintenance Rights of Muslim Women: Principles, Precedents and Trends.* New Delhi: Genuine Publications; 1987.

Waring, Marilyn. *Counting for Nothing: What Men Value and What Women are Worth.* 2nd ed. Toronto: University of Toronto Press. 1999; orig. 1987.

Watts, Charlotte, and Cathy Zimmerman. "Violence Against Women: Global Scope and Magnitude," *The Lancet* 359, no. 9313 (April 6, 2002): 1232–39. Accessed through Proquest, September 2005.

Weiss, Anita. "Within The Walls: Home-Based Work in Lahore." In Eileen Boris and Elisabeth Prügl, eds., *Homeworkers in Global Perspective: Invisible No More.* New York: Routledge, 1996.

Westley, S. B., and Andrew Mason. "Women Are Key Players in the Economies of East and Southeast Asia," *Asia Pacific Population Policy* 44 (January 1998): 1–4. <http://www.ncbi.nlm.nih.gov/entrez/query.fcgi?cmd=Retrieve&db=PubMed&list_uids= 12293729&dopt=Abstrac>

White, Jenny B. *Money Makes Us Relatives: Women's Labor in Urban Turkey.* Austin: University of Texas Press, 1994.

"Women & Gender in Middle East Studies: A Roundtable Discussion," *Middle East Report 205.* <http://www.merip.org/mer/mer205/ellen.htm>

Wong, Edward. "Iraqi Constitution May Curb Women's Rights," *New York Times*, July 20, 2005. <http://www.nytimes.com/2005/07/20/international/middleeast/20women.html?hp&ex=1 121832000&en=09d840d1e4d06041&ei=5094&partner=homepages>

World Bank. *Egypt: Country Gender Assessment.* World Bank. Arab Republic of Egypt, 2003c.

World Bank. *Engendering Development: Policy Research Report.* Washington DC: World Bank, 2002.

World Bank. *Gender and Development in the Middle East and North Africa.* Washington, DC: World Bank, 2004. <http://www.worldbank.org/gender>

World Bank. *Gender and Development in the Middle East and North Africa: Women in the Public Sphere.* Washington, DC: Social and Economic Development Department, 2003b.

World Bank. *Gender Equality and the Millennium Development Goals.* Washington, DC: Gender and Development Group, World Bank, 2003a.

World Bank. *Jobs, Growth, and Governance in the Middle East: Unlocking the Potential for Prosperity.* Washington DC: World Bank, 2003.

World Bank. *Trade, Investment and Development in the MENA: Engaging with the World. [MENA Development Report].* Washington, DC: World Bank, 2003.

World Bank. *Understanding and Responding to Poverty.* Washington DC: World Bank, 2003d.

World Health Organization, Department of Reproductive Health and Research (RHR), *Gender and Health.* Technical paper no. 16, 1998. Reference: WHO/FRH/WHD/98.16. <http://www.who.int/reproductive-health/publications/highlights/highlights_hrp_2004.html>

World Health Organization. *Female Genital Mutilation: A Joint WHO/UNICEF/UNFPA Statement.* Geneva: WHO, 1997.

Wynn, Lisa. "Marriage Contracts and Women's Rights in Saudi Arabia." Pages106–21 in Homa Hoodfar, ed., *Shifting Boundaries in Marriage and Divorce in Muslim Communities.* Montpelier, France: Women Living Under Muslim Laws, 1996.

Young, William C., and Seteney Shami. "Anthropological Approaches to the Arab Family: An Introduction," *Journal of Comparative Family Studies* 28, no. 2 (Summer 1997): 1–13.

Yount, K. M. "Women's Family Power and Gender Preference in Minya, Egypt." *Journal of Marriage and Family.* 67 (May 2005): 410–28.

Yuksel, Sahika. "A Comparison of Violent and Non-Violent Families." In Sirin Tekeli, ed., *Women in Modern Turkish Society: A Reader.* London: Zed Books, 1995.

Zandvakili, Sourushe. "Analysis of Sex-Based Inequality: Use of Axiomatic Approach in Measurement and Statistical Inference Via Bootstrapping." In Mine Cinar, ed., *The Economics of Women and Work in the Middle East and North Africa.* Amsterdam: JAI Press, 2001.